How Indians Really Lived

Through detection and deduction, modern archaeologists and anthropologists have reconstructed the daily life of the first men to inhabit North America. Here is the story of the American Indian, how he worked and worshipped, how he hunted, played, fought, and how he communicated.

Scene at top depicts life in an early Algonkian village. (Photo, after a painting, courtesy of the American Museum of Natural History.) Scene at right is an Arapaho camp of skin-covered tipi of about 1870. (Photo courtesy of the Bureau of American Ethnology, Smithsonian Institution.) Scene below is a painted house front of Bella Coola Indians, British Columbia. (Photo courtesy of the American Museum of Natural History.)

A SCIENCE SURVEY BOOK

HOW INDIANS REALLY LIVED

BY GORDON C. BALDWIN

G.P. Putnam's Sons New York

To Malcolm Reiss
in appreciation

BOOKS BY GORDON C. BALDWIN

AMERICA'S BURIED PAST
THE WORLD OF PREHISTORY
THE ANCIENT ONES
STONE AGE PEOPLES TODAY
THE WARRIOR APACHES
THE RIDDLE OF THE PAST
RACE AGAINST TIME
STRANGE PEOPLES AND STRANGER CUSTOMS
HOW INDIANS REALLY LIVED
INDIANS OF THE SOUTHWEST

Fifth Impression

© 1967 by Gordon C. Baldwin
All Rights Reserved
Published simultaneously in the Dominion of
Canada by Longmans Canada Limited, Toronto
Library of Congress Catalog Card
Number: 67-14801
Printed in the United States of America
12216

Contents

Illustrations

6

How Indians Really Lived

Acknowledgments

I should like to express my thanks and appreciation to the following individuals and institutions for their cooperation in providing illustrations and information for this book:

Dr. Gordon F. Ekholm, Curator of Mexican Archaeology, American Museum of Natural History; Dr. Henry B. Collins. Acting Director of the Bureau of American Ethnology, Smithsonian Institution; Dr. Emil W. Haury, Director of the Arizona State Museum; Miss Wilma Kaemlein of the Arizona State Museum; Merrill J. Mattes, Regional Chief, Division of History and Archeology, National Park Service, Omaha; Dr. Jesse D. Jennings, Professor of Anthropology, University of Utah; Bureau of Indian Affairs, United States Department of the Interior; Department of Citizenship and Immigration, Indian Affairs Branch, Canada; and the Department of Northern Affairs and National Resources, Canada.

1

New World Explorers

LESS THAN five hundred years ago Christopher Columbus sailed across the Atlantic Ocean and discovered the New World. He named its brown-skinned inhabitants Indians, mistakenly thinking he had landed at the East Indies' back door. In spite of this error the name has stuck.

We know now that Columbus was not the first to discover America. Norse seafarers had beaten the Genoan by a good five centuries. But the Norsemen didn't have the press agents that Columbus had, and their explorations went more or less unnoticed until recent years.

Yet even the Norsemen were latecomers. Perhaps 20,-000 years earlier, some unknown, unsung ancestors of the American Indians had crossed over Bering Strait from Asia to Alaska to become the real discoverers of the New World. Their feat, however, like that of the Vikings, didn't make the headlines.

Even today the Indian generally receives little mention in our history books. He is lucky if he gets a whole chapter to himself at the beginning of the book, with perhaps a few later paragraphs about his activities during the French and Indian Wars, the Custer massacre, and similar frontier escapades of the eighteenth and nineteenth centuries.

Back 25,000 years ago neither Siberia nor Alaska looked like they do today. The world was in the tag end of a great ice age that had covered much of the northern hemisphere with ice sheets hundreds and thousands of feet thick. Geologists estimate that so much seawater was stored up in snow and ice that the ocean level was lowered at least two or three hundred feet. This would have been more than enough to expose the shallow, fifty-six-mile stretch of sea bottom connecting the two continents at what is now Bering Strait. The first American immigrants could then easily have walked across dry-shod.

Paleontologists tell us that, thousands of years earlier, the mammoth, giant bison, musk-ox, giant elk and other Asiatic animals migrated to America by just such a land bridge.

The first human arrivals may well have been hot on the trail of their dinner when they made their way across Bering Strait. It is more than likely that they were following one of these big-game mammals. There was enough meat on its bones to feed a small band of hunters for a long time.

We know these people were hunters and fishermen because, at that time, everyone in the whole wide world made their living by hunting or fishing or gathering wild plants. Farming wouldn't be discovered for another 15,000 years.

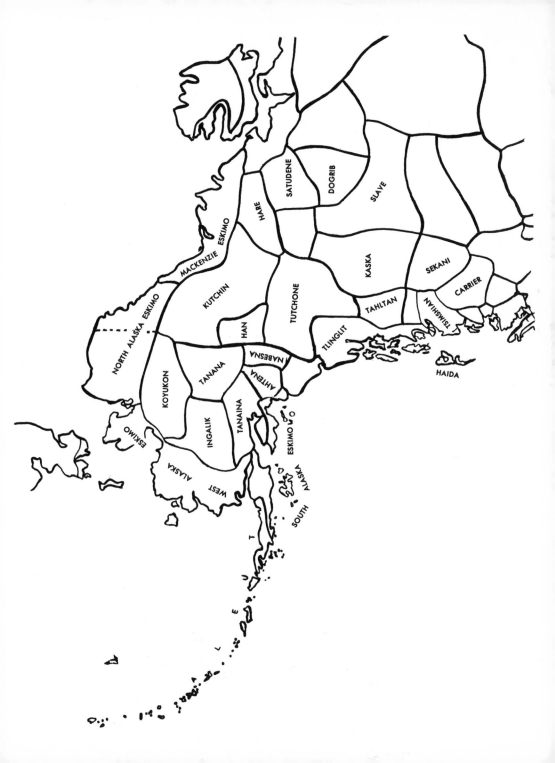

We don't know why these Asiatic hunters left their homeland in Siberia and migrated to America. Probably there were many different reasons. Some may have been crowded out by more numerous and warlike bands of nomads moving up from the south and west. Others may have just wanted to see what lay on the far side of the next mountain range.

Whatever the reason, this first little band of Asiatic hunters crossed Bering Strait and became the discoverers of a new world. They didn't know they were setting foot on a brand-new continent, the last to be discovered. Even if they had known, they couldn't have cared less. All they were interested in was food enough to stuff their bellies and a fire by which to keep warm.

Archaeologists can't tell us much about these first Americans and how they lived. Remains of bones and tools and shelters and clothing are hard to find after being buried for 25,000 years in the frozen Arctic. Scientists have to guess about what happened. But, as a result of their poking here and digging there, they can make reasonably accurate guesses. You might even call them "educated" guesses.

These firstcomers didn't bring much baggage with them. They couldn't afford to own too much because they had to carry everything on their backs or in their hands.

Living in the Arctic, first in Siberia and then in Alaska, they had to know how to make fire and how to use the skins and furs of the animals they killed as clothing to keep warm. They had to know how to put up crude brush shelters against the cold. Also, they knew how to chip flint and similar stones into simple tools and weapons. Hunting, fishing and gathering wild plants were the only ways they knew to make a living. But they were men who were good at all those skills. They had to be. Hunting and fishing were not sports as they are for us. This was deadly serious business. One mistake could be a man's last.

Most of the animals they hunted were far bigger and stronger than they were. The New World, 25,000 years ago, was a hunter's paradise—mammoth, mastodon, giant bison, giant elk, musk-ox, giant ground sloth, horse, camel, even the giant saber-toothed cat. To hunt such huge animals these first Americans had only the most primitive of weapons—spears, spear throwers, stone knives and, perhaps, wooden clubs and bone daggers.

They didn't even have dogs to help them hunt or to carry some of their possessions. Most archaeologists think that dogs crossed over from Asia thousands of years later with some of the more recent immigrants. Nor did they have the bow and arrow. This implement probably came across from Asia with later peoples.

This first small band of New World adventurers numbered only a few dozen at most. But they weren't alone long. Other northern Asiatic nomads soon followed them across Bering Strait. Some of them began taking to the trail once more, lured southward by the abundance of game.

Luckily for these pioneers the massive ice sheets did not cover all of Alaska and northern Canada. Here and there, along the coasts and up and down the great river

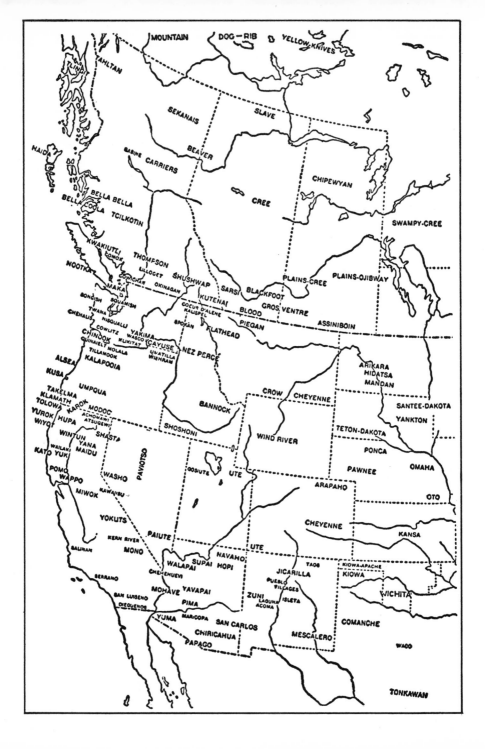

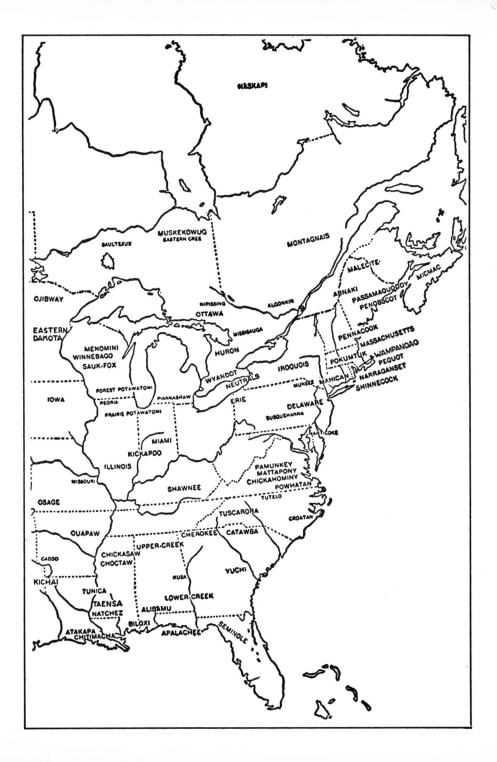

valleys of the Yukon and Mackenzie, were open, ice-free corridors. Through these passages the first Americans wandered, spreading out as they came farther south. They didn't know where they were going. But it didn't matter. It was all new country to them. Ahead of them lay two continents, thousands of acres of uninhabited land, unequaled for hunting and fishing and gathering.

They didn't hurry. Nomadic hunters don't move too many miles in any one day or week. They prefer to hunt and fish and gather in familiar territory. Besides, hunting was hard work. It left little time or energy for other things. Gradually, however, they and their descendants occupied the whole of North, Central and South America. By 14,-000 B.C. some of these big-game hunters had ventured as far south as Venezuela. By 8760 B.C. still others had reached the extreme tip of South America and were toasting giant sloth and horse steaks over their campfires in a Patagonian cave.

So archaeology and carbon 14 dating tells us. Carbon 14 is one of the complicated scientific methods chemists and physicists have developed to help archaeologists date the things they dig up. Carbon 14, heavier than ordinary carbon, is manufactured by cosmic rays bombarding the upper atmosphere. It is present in all living things. When a plant or animal dies, the carbon 14 begins to disintegrate at a fixed rate, being reduced by half in 5,730 years. The date of the ancient bones or charcoal can be determined by comparing the carbon 14 left in them with that in living plants and animals.

Radiocarbon dating also tells us that, about this same

time, other descendants of these Asiatic immigrants were roaming the plains and plateaus of Canada and the United States. Unlike their ancestors, these hunters and seed-gatherers stayed long enough in one place to leave us their broken stone tools and weapons mixed with the ashes of their campfires.

These were the days of Sandia and Clovis and Folsom and Plainview and a dozen other different groups of hunters. Archaeologists named these groups after the different styles of spear points they used to down big game.

While these hunters were pursuing their next meal along

Courtesy, Bureau of American Ethnology, Smithsonian Institution

Fluted Folsom spear points used by early Indians to kill bison and other big game animals

Danger Cave, Utah, the home of early Indians of the Great Basin

the high plains east of the Rocky Mountains, other groups of early Indians were doing the same thing west of the mountains. But there weren't many big mammals in this plateau and mountain country, and the people had to gather seeds and scavenge after whatever small game they could find.

At Tule Springs, near Las Vegas, Nevada, seed-gatherers were hard at work as early as 11,000 B.C. A thousand or two years later other seed-gatherers were camped in Danger Cave, Utah, trying to scrounge a living out of the desert plants and animals. A little later a similar way of life, called Cochise by the archaeologists, was functioning in southern Arizona and New Mexico and northern Mexico.

In the eastern United States by 7000 B.C. many of the Indians had begun to depend on shellfish for a living. As monuments to their appetites, they left behind them huge mounds of empty shells scattered all along the seacoasts and the banks of the larger rivers. Other eastern Indians, however, remained hunters and fishermen.

Shortly after this, perhaps somewhere between 5000 and 7000 B.C., the Ice Age finally came to an end. With the

Courtesy, University of Utah

Prehistoric Indian shell heap near the Potomac River, Maryland

glaciers melting and with grassy plains and forests spreading northward after the retreating ice, you might think that the Indians would have had an easier time of making a living. But you would be wrong.

For thousands of years America had been a paradise for hunters. Then, mysteriously, the huge animals disappeared. Almost overnight they became extinct.

Scientists don't know exactly why this happened. Half a dozen different theories—climatic changes brought about by the end of the Ice Age, disease, famine, volcanic upheavals, even man himself—have been proposed.

Whatever the cause, the close of the Ice Age and the extinction of most of the big-game animals greatly changed the lives of the Indians. For one thing, as the ice melted, the sea level rose and covered the land bridge connecting Siberia and Alaska. Immigrants to the New World now either had to walk across on the ice in winter or navigate crude rafts or skin boats over the open water in summer.

But, what was far more important, the Indians were now forced to depend more and more on wild plant foods. In time, perhaps by accident, perhaps by experimentation, some of these Indians discovered how to plant and raise crops.

Archaeologists, along with botanists and other plant specialists, don't know exactly when and where this happened. Most of them think farming was discovered two or three times in two or three different places with two or three different plants. They have pinned the discoveries down to Mexico, Central America and northern South America. The time was probably somewhere around

5000 B.C., perhaps even a thousand or two thousand years earlier. This was a few thousand years later than similar discoveries in the Old World in southwestern and southeastern Asia.

But these New World farmers were original. They didn't grow the same crops as our remote ancestors cultivated in Asia, for the simple reason that they had never heard of them. The Indians had to find their own wild plants and domesticate them.

Thus, instead of wheat and barley and rye, the Indians discovered and developed corn (maize), potatoes, tomatoes, beans, manioc, squashes and nearly a hundred other food plants. While we can't prove it, the first farmers were probably women. Since the plow was unknown in the New World until it was introduced by the Spaniards and other Europeans, these Indian farmers had to do all their planting and cultivating by hand.

From Mexico, several of these food plants were traded northward into what is now the United States. First to come was corn, probably by way of the ancient, seed-gathering Cochise people of southern New Mexico and Arizona. Still later, beans and squash followed the same path. Along with corn, these plants quickly spread over the eastern United States, reaching as far north as the climate would allow them to be grown.

Unlike the Old World residents, the American Indians had no large animals which they could domesticate. They had to be content with the llama, alpaca and guinea pig far down in the Andean area of South America, and the turkey and the bee in the Southwest and Mexico.

Pottery also spread from Mexico northward into the United States. In the Northeast this native pottery met pottery of a totally different style, called Woodland, which had seemingly been brought over from Siberia by late-arriving immigrants.

With the coming of farming and pottery-making, many of the Indians now changed from nomadic hunters to settled village dwellers. The small Indian villages of Mexico, Central America and South America soon grew into towns and cities. Eventually, there arose the great city-states or empires of the Mayas, Aztecs, Incas and their neighbors.

The northern Indians never reached the heights attained

Courtesy, Arizona State Museum

Broken Flute Cave in northeastern Arizona, the home of Basket Maker Indians

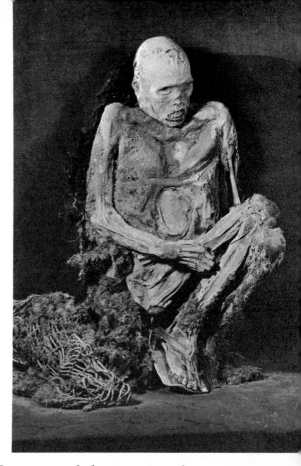

Courtesy, American Museum of
Natural History
Mummy from Canyon del Muerto,
northeastern Arizona

by their southern relatives. But some of them managed to do pretty well for themselves.

Everyone has read about or seen pictures of the ancient cliff dwellings of Arizona, New Mexico and Colorado. These multistoried, stone apartment houses were built nearly a thousand years ago by the Pueblo Indians.

Through the science of reading tree rings, discovered by an Arizona astronomer, archaeologists are able to date these cliff dwellings and also the remains of the ancestors of the Pueblo Indians, the still earlier Basket Makers.

In southeastern Arizona and New Mexico lived the

Mogollon peoples. They were the descendants of some of the Cochise people, who had acquired a knowledge of farming and pottery-making from the Indians of Mexico. They in turn passed that knowledge on to their northern neighbors, the late Basket Makers.

Contemporaneous with the Mogollon Indians, as well as with the Basket Makers and later Pueblo Indians, another people, the Hohokam, inhabited the desert valleys of southern Arizona. They were great farmers, building hundreds of miles of irrigation ditches to water their fields of corn, beans, squashes and cotton.

In the northeastern United States similar changes were taking place. After the Woodland Indians got pottery, possibly from Siberia, and farming by way of Mexico, they began building burial mounds. The idea for these mounds, like that for pottery, may have been brought over by Asiatic immigrants about 1000 B.C.

Archaeologists named some of these earlier mound-builders Adena, and later ones Hopewell, after a couple of mound sites in Ohio. In addition to burial mounds in all sizes and shapes, these people beat chunks of native copper into elaborate breastplates and ornaments and carved stone into statues and tobacco pipes.

About A.D. 500, the Indians in the southeastern United States also began building mounds. These were not the usual burial mounds but huge, flat-topped pyramids serving as bases for temples or other religious buildings. Archaeologists believe that, like farming, the idea for these was borrowed from Mexico. These Temple Mound builders were great manufacturers of decorative ornaments and pieces of pottery and ceremonial objects. They spread northward into the Adena-Hopewell area, building a huge hundred-foot-high mound in what is now East St. Louis, Illinois.

Contrary to what many people believe, these mound-builders were not a mysterious race who disappeared long before the Indians arrived. They were just more Indians. Some of them were still putting up mounds when Spanish explorers visited them in the sixteenth century.

But we are getting ahead of our story.

2

Indians, Indians, Indians

TO MOST people the standard Indian is the one pictured on the old buffalo nickel. If he isn't dressed in beaded buckskin clothing topped by a feathered warbonnet and isn't carrying a tomahawk in one hand and a carved peace pipe in the other, then he isn't an Indian.

This is not true. There is no typical American Indian just as there is no typical twentieth-century American. Indians differ among themselves, both in looks and dress. America was a melting pot long before the flood of European immigrants in the nineteenth century brought the term into existence.

We can't tell what the first American settlers looked like. They didn't stay long enough in any one place to leave us any of their bones. From a few scraps of evidence, however, anthropologists think the earlier immigrants probably looked less Mongoloid than did later arrivals. Some anthropologists even think the first immigrants were not Mongoloids at all but early varieties of Caucasoids, perhaps like the aboriginal Australian blackfellows or the hairy Ainu of Japan.

As some of the Indians became farmers and settled down in villages, they also established graveyards. Archaeologists found the graveyards, and as a result have more bones of these later Indians than of their predecessors.

They soon found that some Indians were tall, some short. Some were slight, others stocky or broad-boned. Some had long and narrow skulls, others broad or round heads. Some had hawklike noses, others straight or concave noses. Some were broad-faced, others narrower-faced.

The Indians were, in fact, a mixed people. This is just what we would expect if the New World was populated, as most archaeologists believe, by small bands crossing Bering Strait from Asia over a period of thousands of years.

Yet practically all Indians have some things in common—brown or reddish-brown skin, straight black hair, sparse beard and body hair, dark eyes, and generally broad cheekbones. Because of these basic features today's American Indians, the descendants of these Ice Age Americans, are classed as members of the Mongoloid, or yellow, race.

Indian languages show this same wide diversity. All Indians do not speak the same language. When Columbus rediscovered America, there were at least two hundred or more different languages spoken by Indians living in America north of Mexico. Although many of these languages, including the people who spoke them, are now extinct, over one hundred are still used daily by thousands of present-day Indians.

These languages were not simple or primitive. They were not made up of animal-like grunts or hand signs. In their grammatical structure they were fully as complicated as our own.

Some Indians, particularly in the Plains area, used sign language. But that was only for purposes of trade or exchange of information between members of tribes speaking different languages. It wasn't because they lacked the words.

Many of us think of Indian languages as having only a few hundred or so words. Actually, the vocabulary of any language depends upon how complex are the lives of the people speaking that language. Though English may have hundreds of thousands of words in an unabridged dictionary, most of us use only a fraction of them. All Indian languages so far studied have words running into the thousands. The Dakota, or Sioux, to name only one, had over 19,000 words.

All these hundreds of Indian languages can be grouped into what linguists call families. A family is a group of related languages. That doesn't mean that people who speak related languages can understand each other. Generally they can't. Our own English language, for example, belongs to the Indo-European family. This includes, in addition to English, Dutch, German, Norwegian, French, Spanish, Italian, Greek, Polish, Russian, Persian, Hindustani, Bengali and a number of other languages. Unless we English-speaking people study these other Indo-European languages, we can't speak them or understand them.

At the time of Columbus, some of the fifty-odd American Indian language families in America north of Mexico were spoken by only a few hundred people. Others were spoken by thousands, extending almost clear across the continent. The largest and most important of these Indian language families are listed below (these, together with the principal tribes in each, are also shown in the accompanying chart):

Algonkian—In 1500, this, the largest of the Indian language families, was spoken by over 192,000 Indians from Hudson Bay south to Virginia and west through the Great Lakes region into the Plains area.

Eskimo—spoken by nearly 90,000 people inhabiting the Arctic Coast from the Aleutian Islands eastward through Canada to Labrador and Greenland.

Siouan—spoken by over 88,000 people who lived mainly west of the Mississippi River in the Plains.

Iroquoian—spoken by over 71,000 Indians from the Gulf of St. Lawrence to Lake Erie and southward into Virginia and the Carolinas.

Muskogean—spoken by over 66,000 people who lived in the southeastern United States.

Aztec-Tanoan—spoken by 63,000 people from the Great Basin southward into Mexico.

Athabascan—spoken by more than 60,000 Indians in northwestern Canada, the Southwest and the Pacific Coast.

Salishan—spoken by nearly 60,000 people in the plateau country of British Columbia, Washington, Idaho and Montana and along the north Pacific Coast.

If you add the above population figures, you should come up with 690,000 people. The other nearly fifty language families are all considerably smaller and only add another 310,000 Indians. This makes a grand total of one million Indian residents of North America north of Mexico when Columbus landed. The rest of the New World—Mexico, Central America and South America was much more densely inhabited, with an estimated Indian population of ten million.

Indian Language Families

ALGONKIAN	ALGONKIAN (*continued*)	IROQUOIAN
Atlantic Woodlands	Gros Ventre	Northeastern Woodlands
Abnaki	Piegan	Cayuga
Algonkian	Plains Cree	Erie
Delaware		Huron or Wyandot
Massachusetts	ESKIMO	Mohawk
Micmac	Aleut	Neutrals
Montagnais	Eskimo	Onondaga
Narraganset		Seneca
Naskapi		Susquehanna
Pequot	SIOUAN	Southeastern Woodlands
Powhatan	Plains	Cherokee
Wampanoag	Assiniboine	Tuscarora
Great Lakes Area	Crow	
Cree	Dakota (Sioux)	MUSKOGEAN
Illinois	Hidatsa	Southeastern Area
Kickapoo	Iowa	Alibama
Menominee	Kansa	Apalachee
Miami	Mandan	Calusa
Ojibway	Omaha	Chickasaw
Ottawa	Osage	Choctaw
Potawatomi	Oto	Creek
Sauk and Fox	Ponca	Natchez
Shawnee	Southerners	Seminole
Plains Country	Biloxi	
Arapaho	Catawba	AZTEC-TANOAN
Blackfoot	Quapaw	Southwest
Blood	Northerners	Hopi
Cheyenne	Winnebago	New Mexico Pueblos

AZTEC-TANOAN (*cont.*)	ATHABASCAN (*cont.*)	SALISHAN
Papago	Hare	Plateau
Pima	Slave	Flathead
Plateau	Tanana	Kalispel
Bannock	Yellowknife	Spokane
Paiute	North Pacific Coast	Wenatchi
Shoshoni	Haida	Okanagon
Snake	Tlingit	Shuswap
Ute	Tsimshian	Coast
Wind River	California	Bellacoola
California	Hupa	Chehalis
Mission Tribes	Kato	Nisqualli
Mono	Tolowa	Squamish
Plains	Plains	Tillamook
Comanche	Kiowa-Apache	
Kiowa	Sarsi	CADDOAN
	Southwest	Arikara
ATHABASCAN	Navaho	Pawnee
Alaska and Canada	Western Apache	Wichita
Beaver	Jicarilla	
Carrier	Lipan	
Chipewyan	Chiricahua	
Dogrib	Mescalero	

These figures are, of course, only estimates or educated guesses made by anthropologists. There were no census-takers in those days to make an accurate count.

These million North American Indians were divided into some three hundred different tribes. We often hear the term "tribe" used, but not many of us know just what it means. A tribe is simply a group of people having a common language, a common name for themselves, and claiming a definite territory. Some have some form of government, but others have little or none.

Indian tribes varied greatly in size. Some had as few as fifty or a hundred people. Others numbered into the thousands. Probably most tribes counted less than a thousand members, including both old and young.

The names by which we know most Indian tribes are not usually those given to them by the Indians themselves. They are generally English, French or Spanish translations of native names or nicknames applied by one tribe to another. Actually, many tribes call themselves simply "the people" or "the men" or something similar to show that they consider themselves set apart from all other peoples.

The Navaho Indians in Arizona and New Mexico, for example, call themselves Dene, the People. The name Navaho was given them by some of the neighboring Pueblo Indians.

Anthropologists, scientists of the study of man, like to classify things, to file them neatly away in pigeonholes. We saw an illustration of this in the way they put each Indian tribe into its proper language family. They do the same with Indian culture.

Culture has a lot of different meanings. To us it often means such things as music and dancing and drama and similar arts. But to an anthropologist it means the way of life of a tribe or group of people—how they live, the tools they make, the ceremonies and rituals they practice, even how and what they think.

Like the people of the rest of the world, Indians were not all alike in their culture, in the way they lived. Some Indians depended upon hunting or fishing for their living, others on gathering wild plants, still others on farming. Some Indians lived in tipis, others in log huts, still others in stone apartment houses. Some were rich in material goods; others had a hard time keeping the wolf from the door.

This doesn't mean that some Indians were a lot smarter than others. So far as we know, they were not. Many Indians owed their good fortune to their nearness to the higher Indian civilizations in Mexico, whose achievements could be easily borrowed and suited to their own needs. Some had settled on land where the climate was right for farming. Others ended up on land where farming was impossible. Still others were located on the fringes of the continent, where they were completely out of touch with higher developments and could only borrow ideas and techniques from neighbors who were not much better off than they were.

Anthropologists soon discovered that, like language, Indian culture could also be classified and put in pigeonholes. They called these pigeonholes "culture areas."

A culture area is a geographic region within which all or most of the tribes share much the same kind of life, a life differing from that followed by tribes in adjoining regions. In each of these areas, houses and clothing and tools and religious beliefs and all the other things that go to make up a way of life are more or less alike.

This similarity in culture comes about because Indian tribes, like any other peoples including ourselves, are always borrowing items and ideas from other tribes living close to them.

It is also due to the nature of the resources of the culture area. Culture areas roughly correspond to large geographic regions—the eastern woodlands, the grassy plains, the southwestern desert country. Each area differs from the others in physiography, in climate and in plants and animals. The Indians were quick to take advantage of what Nature had provided them and adapted or adjusted their culture to the environment in which they lived. Thus, you would not be surprised to find birchbark canoes and houses in the woodlands. But you would be astonished if they turned up in the Arizona desert.

Anthropologists also discovered that there was no sharp break or dividing line between two adjacent culture areas. Tribes near the center of a given area showed similar cultures typical of that area. But those on the outskirts had picked up foreign cultural elements from their neighbors in the next area. Along the borders, then, there was an overlap, with the two ways of life tending to blend into each other.

In spite of this, the culture area is a convenient method of describing how most of the people in a particular region lived. A description of only one tribe serves as a description of the twenty or thirty tribes living in that culture area.

Anthropologists have identified nine of these culture areas in prehistoric America north of Mexico—Arctic, Mackenzie-Yukon, Northwest Coast, California, Basin-Plateau, Southwest, Plains, Northeastern Woodlands, and Southeastern Woodlands.

Following this scheme, we shall try to describe Indian ways of life as they were in the sixteenth, seventeenth, and eighteenth centuries, in the days before most of the tribes were uprooted and displaced by European explorers and settlers.

3

Farmers and Woodsmen of the Northeast

I T IS fitting that we begin our survey of the American Indian with the farmers and woodsmen of the Northeastern Woodlands area. For these were the Indians who played such a prominent role in the early history of our country.

These were the Indians who may have greeted the first European explorers to venture across the Atlantic, the Norsemen. Six hundred years later their descendants met the Pilgrim Fathers at Plymouth Rock. They taught the Pilgrims how to plant corn with fishheads as fertilizer, how to harvest maple syrup, how to make birchbark canoes.

These were also among the first Indian tribes to face the relentless westward tide of land-hungry English, Dutch and French settlers. But bows and arrows and war clubs were no match against firearms. As a result, most of these Indian tribes are now extinct. Their deeds are preserved for us in James Fenimore Cooper's novels *The Last of the Mohicans* and *The Deerslayer*.

This was the homeland of such famous Indian leaders

and statesmen as Massasoit, the Wampanoag chieftain who befriended the Pilgrims, and his son, King Philip. Here lived the real Hiawatha, a Mohawk Indian chief; Powhatan and his daughter, Pocahontas, of Virginia fame; Tammany, the Delaware Indian chief whose name has come down to us in New York's Tammany Hall; Red Jacket, the Seneca chief; Pontiac, the famous chief of the Ottawas; and Tecumseh, the Shawnee war leader.

The Northeastern Woodlands culture area was a big one, extending from Hudson Bay and Labrador southward along the Atlantic Coast to Virginia and westward through the Great Lakes and the Ohio River valley to the Mississippi River.

Half a millenium ago this was even more woodland country than it is today. Thick forests of ash, elm, oak, hemlock, birch and maple covered the rolling hills and valleys. There were springs, streams, rivers and lakes. The woods were full of all kinds of birds and animals and wild food plants, and the rivers and lakes equally full of fish. The ground was fertile and the climate, except in the far north, suitable for farming.

Most of the dozens of Indian tribes in this area spoke Algonkian languages. The only important exception was the Iroquoian tribes of New York and the shores of Lake Erie.

Anthropologists estimate that there were a little more than 200,000 Indians living in this Northeastern Woodlands area just before the European invasion began. Nearly half of these lived around the Great Lakes, with over 100,000 occupying the remainder of the area.

The far north had, as you would expect, the smallest population. The Algonkian tribes in this northern country, the Cree, Ojibway, Montagnais, and Naskapi, were mainly nomadic hunters and fishermen. Lacking the farming, pottery and basketry of their southern relatives, their culture was, in many respects, much like that of the Indians of the Mackenzie culture area farther to the north and west.

In the rest of the area, however, the Indians were farmers. Nearly every village had its garden, with those of the Iroquoian tribes generally being the largest. Sometimes two or three hundred acres of cultivated land might surround a single village. Fields were cleared of trees and brush by cutting and burning. As garden tools the Indian women used simple wooden digging sticks or equally simple hoes made from the shoulder blades of deer or sharpened tortoiseshell, or stone.

Corn was the principal crop, including both starchy corn and flint corn, as well as sweet corn and popcorn. The Indians also planted beans, squashes, pumpkins, sunflowers and tobacco.

Tobacco was widely used by both the Algonkian and Iroquoian tribes. It was often mixed with other plants such as sumac leaves and dogwood bark. Such mixtures in the eastern United States and Canada were called kinnikinnik, from an Algonkian word meaning "mixed." Tobacco was smoked in straight or elbow-shaped pipes of clay or stone, with wood or reed stems. Smoking played an important part in almost every ceremony.

The Indians were ingenious when it came to methods

of cooking, drying or preserving foods. They cut up squashes and pumpkins into strips, dried them and stored them away in underground pits lined with skins or bark. They parched or dried corn and stored it in bark barrels or hung it up in bunches in the houses. There were over fifty different recipes alone for the serving of corn. These ranged from corn on the cob to roasted ears, hominy, mush, popcorn, corn bread, johnycake, puddings, succotash and all kinds of corn soup.

Yet the wealth of this area lay in its forests. The influence of woods and lakes and rivers is evident in almost every phase of Indian life. In many tribes farming played second fiddle to hunting, fishing and gathering. Men hunted deer, bear, moose, beaver, rabbits and such wild fowl as turkey, quail and ducks. Sturgeon and other fish were caught in the lakes and rivers with hooks, nets, spears and traps. In winter the Indians chopped holes in the lake ice to spear fish.

Wild vegetable products were important articles of diet throughout the area. In the upper Great Lakes, the Menominee, Ojibway and Winnebago Indians annually harvested the wild rice growing along the marshy shores of lakes and rivers.

Wherever sugar maples grew, the Indians tapped them in the spring for their maple syrup, boiling down the sap and hardening it in molds. A particular family's right to use certain groups of sugar maples was handed down from generation to generation.

Many of these Algonkian and Iroquoian foods were adopted by the early European settlers. Some of them are still favorite foods—popcorn, hominy, succotash, maple sugar, wild rice and persimmon bread, to name only a few.

Most of these Algonkian and Iroquoian tribes lived in small to large villages in the forests or on the shores of lakes and rivers. The Indian was never far from trees. From the woodlands came the raw materials for his home, his canoe, his tools and weapons, his cooking utensils.

The term wigwam is an Algonkian word for house. The typical wigwam was circular or oval in ground plan, made of a framework of saplings set in the ground and bent over and tied at the top in a dome shape. Over this were laid slabs of birchbark or, occasionally, cattail-stalk mats tied or pegged in place. A doorway was left in one side and a smoke hole in the roof. Bark platforms around the sides were used as seats by day and beds by night.

The Iroquois didn't build wigwams. As their name suggests, "The People of the Longhouse," they lived in large community houses. The characteristic Iroquois house was a rectangular building twenty or thirty feet in both width and heighth and from fifty to one hundred and fifty feet long. It was built of an arching pole framework covered with flat slabs of birchbark. Down the center ran a corridor for the fires of the numerous families who lived in separate rooms on either side. At each end was a small lobby for the storage of firewood and an outside door of bark or skin. As in Algonkian wigwams, bark platforms raised a foot or two above the earthen floor served each family both as seats and beds.

In size, Iroquoian villages ranged from three hundred to three thousand inhabitants. Each village was fortified by a surrounding trench and a palisade of high, sharp-pointed logs. Many of the Algonkian villages were also palisaded against enemy attack.

The animals of the forest furnished the Indian with his clothing. Nearly everything he wore was made of tanned deerskin sewn with deer sinew. In the summer a man wore breechcloth and moccasins of soft dressed deerskin. A belt around the waist held the foot-wide skin breechcloth in place. In winter he added a pair of buckskin-fringed, knee-length leggings and a fur robe of rabbit or bear skins. Some men wore sleeved shirts or jackets of buckskin.

Moccasins and tailored skin or fur garments probably reached the New World by way of Bering Strait. Some archaeologists believe these two inventions, along with the bow and arrow, may have been brought over by Athabascan-speaking immigrants who arrived not too many centuries before the beginning of the Christian Era.

The Indian woman didn't wear any more clothing than a man. In warm weather her costume consisted of a pair of soft deerskin moccasins and a rectangular piece of deerskin long enough to reach from her waist to below the knees. A skin belt held this wraparound slit skirt in place. In colder weather she added a fur robe. During the first ten years of their lives children went around nude.

The clothing of both men and women was often decorated with designs of dyed porcupine quills and moose hair. As soon as the European traders brought in glass beads, these quickly replaced quill decoration. Although beads were at first sewn on deerskin, cloth was shortly obtained from the traders and beads were sewn on this in elaborate floral patterns.

Women let their hair grow long, often gathering it into a thick beaver tail or ponytail hanging down the back of the head. Bear fat was used as a hair dressing. As cold cream, the Indian women used fish oil and eagle fat. They also painted their faces with bright red pigment, sometimes outlining the eyes with black paint. Paints were made by grinding up minerals or by boiling the sap from certain plants. These were usually mixed with bear fat or sunflower oil for easier spreading.

The Indian men, however, would have made beauty-parlor operators rich. Men were liberal in their use of face and body paint, frequently painting themselves with ornamental figures of birds and animals over a colored background. Like the women, they carried make-up kits containing little bags of paints and fat.

The Indian man paid even more attention to his hair than did his wife. He dressed it daily with bear fat to make it shiny and glossy, sometimes mixing in soot to add to its blackness.

But his crowning glory was the peculiar fashion in which he, together with many of his fellow northeastern Indian men, wore his hair. This was shaved or cut close on either side of the head, leaving a ridge of close-cropped hair standing up like a cockscomb from front to back. At the back of the head the hair on this ridge was left long and was braided into what has been called a scalp lock. To make the ridge of upstanding hair even more conspicuous

Courtesy, American Museum of Natural History

Model of Iroquois warrior

some Indians wore artificial cockscombs or roaches of deer bristles or of moose hair. These artificial wigs were sometimes dyed bright red.

Everyone has heard the word wampum. This is a New England Algonkian term meaning "strings of shell beads." In addition to paint and fancy headgear, most Northeastern Indians wore some kind of shell ornaments. This jewelry was probably what the word wampum originally meant to the Indians. But that soon changed once the Dutch and English arrived in New York and New England early in the seventeenth century.

These colonists had little money and soon began to use shell beads as a medium of exchange. With the aid of iron tools the Indians were able to turn out these purple and white cylindrical shell beads by the thousands. They were generally made from the common hardshell clam called quahog. The laws of the colonies even fixed the value of wampum. It was often handled in units known as fathoms, 360 white or 180 purple beads making a fathom. Purple beads were twice as valuable as white beads, averaging about five to the penny.

The Indians made and used vast quantities of wampum to pay tribute demanded by the settlers. Five hundred thousand beads were frequently asked for and received.

But the most famous objects made of wampum were the ceremonial belts, particularly those of the Iroquois. White signified peace, purple was the sign of mourning, red of war.

Like their clothing and houses, most of the implements and utensils of these Indians came from the forest. House-

Courtesy, Bureau of American
Ethnology, Smithsonian Institution
Iroquois wampum records

hold furnishings included woven mats of rushes, bark or corn husks for sitting and sleeping, wooden mortars and pestles for pounding their corn into meal, and baskets woven of corn husks, rushes and wooden splints. From the inner bark of certain trees they made thread and cord by shredding and twisting the fiber and rolling it back and forth with the palm of the hand on the thigh. With this thread they wove belts, headbands, burden straps and rectangular bags.

Even though these Northeastern Woodlands Indians had only primitive stone, bone and shell tools, they were excellent wood-carvers and carpenters. They carved wood into spoons, ladles, bowls and canoe paddles. But most of the Indians preferred bark to wood. Out of bark they made a variety of such household articles as ladles, bowls, dishes, trays, tubs, boxes and barrels. Bark dishes, when bent into shape and sewn together with thread, with the seams coated with spruce gum, were watertight enough to serve as cooking vessels. Many Indians, however, made red or buff or gray pottery vessels for both cooking and storage. Many of these were cord-marked, pointed-bottom clay pots that may have been introduced from Asia. Others, like those of the Iroquoian tribes, had rounded bottoms and flaring rims decorated with incised designs of dots and lines.

The Indians manufactured ground and polished stone axes, hammers, chipped flint knives and scrapers, and arrowheads and spearheads. From animal bone and horn they made awls, needles, punches, knives and combs.

For transportation of themselves and their baggage, the Indians used either their own feet or canoes. They had dogs but chose to fatten them up for food or use them in hunting rather than use them for pack animals. With the aid of a tumpline, or burden strap, across the forehead, the Indians could carry good-size loads on their backs.

One of the most practical and ingenious inventions the Woodlands Indians ever made was the birchbark canoe. A multitude of streams, rivers and lakes forming a network of waterways over the entire region made water transportation the easiest and simplest way to get from one place to another. To the Woodlands Indian the birchbark canoe was as necessary as the automobile is to us today.

In the southern part of the area, where birch trees wouldn't grow, the Indians were forced to build the heavier and clumsier dugout canoe. They hollowed this out from a single large tree with fire and stone adzes, scraping away the charred wood until the craft had reached its desired shape.

But wherever they could they used the portable, bark-covered canoe. If birchbark wasn't available, spruce or elm bark was occasionally used. But birchbark was the best. It could be peeled off the tree at any time of the year. It was light and pliable and could be bent over a cedar rib frame. The edges of the bark sheets were perforated and sewn together with spruce root strings. The seams were made watertight with spruce gum.

The Indian was as skillful in handling this canoe as he was in making it. Nor were all of his canoes small. Some were large enough to hold twenty or more men or a cargo of several tons.

In winter, when rivers and lakes were frozen over and the ground was covered with snow, the Indians still managed to get around by using snowshoes or toboggans. These were also Old World inventions that the late-arriving Athabascans brought over from Siberia.

All of this sounds like the Algonkian and Iroquoian tribes in the Northeastern Woodlands led a happy and peaceful life until the Europeans came along and began crowding them out of their homelands.

But this was simply not true.

What was true was that both the Algonkian and Iroquoian braves spent a lot of their spare time fighting. A state of almost perpetual warfare existed between the Algonkian and Iroquoian groups. And when the Algonkian tribes weren't making war against the Iroquois, they were fighting among themselves.

This state of affairs can be partly traced back to the political setup. There were well over fifty different Algonkian tribes. Each of these considered itself a separate little nation, set apart from all the others. Each of these tribes was subdivided into a number of bands. Each band in turn possessed its own territory and was more or less independent of the other bands. Generally there was no tribal chief. Each band or village, however, had its own chief.

Bands or tribes were always quarreling and feuding among themselves as revenge for former injuries or over the theft of a few acres of sugar maples. The fact that the highest honors always went to the most daring warrior didn't help to promote peace. Even though the elders always preached peace, they were at the same time advising the young to be brave and ruthless in warfare. Under these conditions, peace was never possible for long.

Tribal unity was maintained more through ties of language, clan and kinship than through political organization. Like most so-called primitive peoples, these Indians knew their genealogies forwards and backwards. Kinship, one's relationship to others, was what counted in daily life.

The basic social unit, then as now, was the family, consisting of a man and his wife and their children. But these people didn't all think of the family in the same way that we do. We count descent and relationship on both sides of the family, using what may be termed a bilateral system, but these Indians reckoned descent on only one side of the family. A person belonged either to his mother's family or to his father's family, not to both. Anthropologists call such a unilateral method of determining relationship the clan system.

A clan is simply a group of people who are supposedly all descended from a single, remote ancestor. In some tribes this hypothetical ancestor was a male, in others a female, and descent from this hypothetical ancestor was reckoned unilineally. Everyone in the tribe belonged to the particular clan into which he was born. He could not marry a member of his own clan. Thus, in any given family in a clan system based on the male line, a father and his children belonged to one clan, the wife to another.

Depending upon the size of the tribe, there might be from ten to twenty or more clans, each with its own clan chief. Each clan had its own name, usually that of an animal, bird or fish. Ottawa tribal clans, for example, included Bear, Wolf, Wildcat, Beaver, Otter, Mink, Owl, Swan, Crane, Turtle and Sturgeon. Clan symbols representing these figures were frequently painted or engraved on various objects belonging to clan members.

The Iroquoian tribes also had clans, each tracing its descent back to a female ancestor. The woman owned and controlled the house, the household furnishings and the food. The husband lived there, you might say, by sufferance. If he left, he could take nothing with him except his clothing, his weapons and his pipe. The real man of the household was the brother of the wife, since he belonged to the same clan as his sister. According to one authority, the Seneca's clans were Bear, Wolf, Turtle, Beaver, Deer, Snipe, Heron and Hawk.

The name Iroquois usually refers to the six tribes in New York—Seneca, Oneida, Onondaga, Cayuga, Mohawk, and Tuscarora. The Tuscarora, however, were latecomers. In danger of being wiped out in their North Carolina homeland by settlers and their Indian allies, in 1715 they sought refuge among their relatives in New York.

The Iroquois were more politically conscious than the Algonkians. The tribe formed a politial as well as a territorial unit, with a council of chiefs representing the several clans. But the Iroquois went far beyond this. Shortly before the European settlers arrived in the New World, the five Iroquois tribes in New York formed the League of the Five Nations. After the Tuscarora joined them, it was called the Six Nations.

Unique among American Indians north of Mexico, this confederacy is credited to the legendary heroes, Dekanawida and Hiawatha. The league had as its chief purpose the preservation of peace among the five Iroquois tribes. Authority rested in a council of fifty peace chiefs elected by the member tribes. Voting, however, was by tribes, each having one vote. Decisions had to be unanimous. This League of the Iroquois is said to have had a strong influence on the formation by the Thirteen Colonies of our own democratic form of government.

The founding of the League may have meant peace for

the five Iroquois tribes, but it brought bloody warfare to the neighboring Algonkian tribes. Even the Huron and Erie, two large Iroquoian-speaking tribes near the Great Lakes, weren't spared. Anthropologists estimate that one of the biggest Huron towns contained two hundred long-houses in which lived some five thousand Indians. Yet by the time the Iroquois got through with them there were only a few thousand Hurons and Eries left. The remnants moved westward and became known as the Wyandots.

In the later struggle between England and France for the control of North America, the Iroquois sided with the English. That is one reason why North America is now English instead of French.

The Indian technique of fighting was based on ambush and surprise. They specialized in hit-and-run guerrilla-type raids. Small war parties of half a dozen to fifty men were more common than larger armies. The largest war parties were probably those of the Iroquois after the formation of the League. Until the Indians secured firearms and iron tomahawks from the traders, they fought with bows and arrows, wooden- or stone-headed clubs, stone axes, and stone or bone knives. The term tomahawk originally meant the Algonkian war club. Later the word was used to mean the iron-headed hatchet. The practice of scalping wasn't widespread until the Europeans began offering bounties to their Indian allies for scalps of their enemies.

Fighting was a means of gaining honor and prestige. To be considered an adult citizen ready for marriage a young man had to kill an enemy.

Warfare was generally accompanied with a great deal of ceremony. There were ceremonies before the warriors left and victory celebrations when they returned.

Some Indians, but particularly the Iroquois, tortured the prisoners they captured on raids. Children and young men and women might be adopted into the tribe to replace relatives lost in war. But the older men were tied to stakes and tortured by mutilation, being shot with arrows and, finally, burning to death over a slow fire.

There are many misunderstandings and misconceptions about Indian religion. To the Indian, religion was a practical matter touching every part of his daily life. It was designed to help him, not in some dim and distant future, but at the present moment. It was tied in closely with nature. Lacking today's scientific knowledge, the Indians endowed nature and all its phenomena with life, with spirit. They believed all natural objects—plants, animals, rocks, sun, moon, wind, rain, lightning—had supernatural power. The Algonkians called this power Manitou, the Iroquois Orenda. The first European explorers, not fully understanding this belief, translated it as meaning "The Great Spirit."

Just as these Indians had no one chief or ruler in their daily life, they couldn't comprehend the principle of a single ruling deity. They believed in any number of supernatural beings. Some were more important than others and were frequently given names.

There were both good spirits and bad spirits. If an individual were bothered by an evil spirit, he tried to get rid of it by offerings. When things were going well, the good spirits responsible had to be rewarded with gifts or ceremonies.

The Indians also believed in personal supernatural guardian spirits. These were received through dreams, usually after a period of isolation and fasting.

Shamans, or medicine men, were individuals who had a lot of supernatural power. They called on their guardian spirits to help cure disease, to foretell the future, to bring good weather and to insure success in warfare. Their drugstore was the neighboring forest, where they gathered plants from which they brewed many different concoctions. If these medicines didn't work, then the shamans might resort to magic.

But, when it came to healing the sick, the shamans had to take a backseat to secret societies, or medicine lodges. One of the most important such organizations among many Algonkian tribes was the Midewiwin, or Grand Medicine Society. This secret curing society had special songs and rites to help the sick. This society, as well as some clans and individuals, had sacred medicine bundles which they used for ceremonial purposes. These were bags containing fossils, quartz crystals, bird feathers, tobacco and tobacco pipes, carvings and all kinds of charms.

The Iroquois also had their secret curing societies, each with its officials, rituals, songs and sacred paraphernalia, including masks, drums, flutes, whistles and gourd or tortoiseshell rattles. Perhaps the best known is the False Face

Carved wooden mask of the Iroquois False Face Society

Society, which is still operating today. The members of this group wore grotesque masks carved from wood.

In spite of the efforts of shamans and curing societies, people still died. And even in those days the cost of burial was often high. Death called for some sort of ceremony, sometimes simple, sometimes elaborate. The body was usually laid away in a grave, together with the implements and utensils of the deceased. In the far north it was frequently impossible to dig a grave, and the carefully wrapped body was put up in a tree or on high posts.

Among the Hurons there were two burials. When a Huron died, his body was put in a bark coffin and raised up on wooden posts. At ten- or twelve-year intervals the Indians held a great ceremony, The Feast of the Dead. The bones of all the dead were gathered together and dressed in new clothes or put in skin bags. These were then reburied in one mass burial pit along with pottery, tools, weapons and ornaments.

The story of these Northeastern Woodlands Indians is a tragic one, full of broken promises and treaties, massacres of both Indians and whites, bitter struggles over ownership of the land, and the removal by force of the surviving members of most of the tribes.

But that story you can read for yourselves in your history books.

4

Cornplanters of the Southeast

THE SOUTHEASTERN Woodlands culture area was one of the most densely populated regions north of Mexico. Less than half the size of the Northeastern Woodlands, it yet was home to some 185,000 Indians when the first Spanish explorers arrived in the sixteenth century.

The area covered by the Southeastern Woodlands extends south from Virginia and Kentucky to the Gulf of Mexico and westward to, and slightly beyond, the Mississippi River.

Like its sister area to the north, this was formerly woodland country covered with forests of chestnut, walnut, oak, hickory, pine, sycamore and cypress. With the exception of the Appalachian Mountains, the highest land east of the Rocky Mountains, this was rolling country. It had its share of water in streams and rivers. With a warm climate and abundant rainfall, there were few places where crops wouldn't grow.

The Indians who occupied this country were the descendants of the prehistoric mound builders who built temple mounds all over the Southeastern region and even up into the northeastern area. In their arts and crafts, in their complex social and political organization, and in their ceremonial life, these people ranked among the highest of any north of Mexico.

This brilliant Temple Mound culture reached its peak around A.D. 1500 or shortly thereafter. Some archaeologists think it may have already been on the downgrade when De Soto toured through the region in 1540–42. At least about this time there seems to have been a decline in population as well as a decline in the building of temple mounds.

Beginning with the 1513 voyage of Ponce de Leon to Florida, the Southeastern Woodlands received a steady stream of Spanish, French and English visitors. Some, like Ponce de Leon, were greeted with a volley of arrows and departed in a hurry. Some, like Hernando de Soto, came hunting for gold and glory and, instead, wound up six feet under the ground. Others settled down and stayed—the Spanish in Florida, the English in Virginia and the Carolinas, the French along the Mississippi River. In time, these newcomers outnumbered the original inhabitants and began to crowd the Indians off their lands. Finally, in the nineteenth century the Government forcibly removed most of the survivors to reservations west of the Mississippi.

That, in brief, is the history of the Southeastern Woodlands, a history that sounds much the same as that of the area just to the north.

The largest and most important language family in the Southeast was the Muskogean. Typical of the peoples in this family were the tribes forming the great Creek confederacy which spread over most of what is now Georgia and Alabama. Other large Muskogean tribes included the Choctaw of central and southern Mississippi, the Chickasaw of northern Mississippi, the Natchez of southwestern Mississippi, the Apalachee of northern Florida and the Calusa of southern Florida. The latter tribe was the one that gave Ponce de Leon such a hard time.

The largest tribe in the Southeast, however, belonged to the Iroquoian family, not to the Muskogean. This was the Cherokee tribe, which occupied the southern Appalachians from West Virginia to northern Georgia and Alabama. We have already mentioned another Iroquoian tribe, the Tuscarora, who left their home in North Carolina to join relatives in New York.

Speaking Siouan languages were the Biloxi of the Mississippi coast, the Catawba and other tribes in the Carolinas, and the Quapaw in Arkansas.

In addition, there were a great many other tribes belonging to one or another of a half dozen small language families.

In contrast to the generally long-headed Indians of the Northeastern Woodlands, most of these Southeasterners had heads that were broad in proportion to their length.

What makes it difficult to study these tribes is that many of them didn't stay put. During historic days, and seemingly even in late prehistoric times, tribes were splitting apart, combining or disappearing entirely. Others were continually on the move, wandering from this place to that.

The Algonkian Shawnee, for example, moved from the Ohio River valley to Tennessee, to South Carolina, to Pennsylvania, to Ohio and to a half dozen other states before finally winding up in Oklahoma with other Southeastern tribes.

The Muskogean-speaking Seminole, a tribe nearly everyone has heard or read about, didn't even exist until the latter part of the eighteenth and the early nineteenth centuries. It was formed by refugee Creeks and other tribes who joined together in Florida to escape the United States Army. Although the greater part were eventually moved to Oklahoma, several hundred remain today in Florida, still technically at war with the United States.

Even though the culture of these Southeastern Indians may have passed its peak when the first Europeans arrived, it was rich and colorful enough to impress the newcomers. In fact, they called the Cherokee, Choctaw, Chickasaw, Creek and Seminole the Five Civilized Tribes.

Actually, practically all the Southeastern tribes were civilized to the extent that they were farmers and lived in permanent towns and villages.

Most people lived in towns on or near the banks of rivers. Each town centered around a large plaza or square, with from two to a dozen or more mounds arranged about its sides. Clustered around these were the dwellings of the people, with the carefully tended fields radiating out in all directions.

Frequently the town was protected against enemies by a palisade of upright posts. The log palisade around one Creek village was 3,500 feet in length. There might also

Diorama of life in an early Natchez town

be moats or earthen embankments surrounding the village. At the ancient town of Etowah, Georgia, the protecting moat was seventeen feet deep and thirty-five feet wide.

Dominating the town and countryside were the huge, flat-topped mounds. These were built of heaped-up layers of earth and clay, with the outside sometimes faced with a smooth coating of clay. These artificial hills were constructed entirely by hand, of basketful after basketful of earth carried up to the top and dumped. Archaeologists know this because they have found lumps of clay and dirt still bearing the imprint of baskets and woven bags. A ramp or stairway of earth or logs slanted up the side to the top. One early Creek mound near Macon, Georgia, was different. It was circular and had a spiral ramp winding counterclockwise around the mound to the summit.

Some of these mounds rose seventy to eighty feet into the sky and measured five hundred feet square at the base. But most were only ten to thirty or forty feet high. Yet, in a land of low, one-story houses, even these were imposing structures.

They were made still more imposing by the temples and other structures set on their flat tops. We don't know too much about these temples. Mounds last almost forever, but wooden buildings decay in a hurry. Temples seem to have been rectangular in floor plan, constructed of wooden posts and rafters covered with matting or thatch. Walls were frequently plastered with clay. We can guess that the temples were decorated and held altars or other ceremonial objects. We do know that a sacred fire was kept burning in some of them all year long.

Other mounds served as platforms for the large houses of priests and rulers, while the ordinary citizen had to be content with a smaller house down on the ground. Most dwellings were built of such light materials as cane, reeds, palmetto, bark or grass. Sometimes walls were made of upright poles and interlaced reeds plastered over with clay. In some tribes houses were square or rectangular, in others round or dome-shaped. The Creeks and Chickasaws and some of their neighbors had both winter and summer houses. Furniture was scanty, consisting of sleeping platforms covered with cane or rush mats and carved wooden stools.

Some tribes, like the Creeks and Cherokees, built large round council houses which also served as men's clubs and as dance halls for ceremonies.

These Southeastern Indians were farmers. From Virginia to Louisiana the valleys were covered with fields of corn, beans, squashes, pumpkins, sunflowers and tobacco. For planting and cultivating, the women bent their backs over wooden digging sticks and hoes of stone, shell or animal shoulder blades fastened to wooden handles.

In their spare time the women also gathered such wild plant foods as roots, seeds, berries, persimmons and nuts. Meanwhile, the men were out fishing or hunting deer, bear, alligators and turtles. Fish were often caught with hook and line, speared, shot with arrows, netted and trapped. When the water was low in summer, the Indians threw certain plants into the water to drug the fish.

In the warm Southeast the Indians didn't have the need for clothes that their northern cousins did. The men wore only a breechcloth made of buckskin or, in Florida, of braided palm fiber. Except for traveling, when they donned moccasins, most of the time they went barefoot.

The women didn't wear much more. Their normal costume consisted of a short skirt of buckskin or, in Florida, of moss. In cold weather both men and women added heavy robes of bear, otter or beaver skins. To keep their legs warm, men also put on buckskin leggings, while the women merely lengthened their skirts.

Rulers, priests, nobles and other high-ranking individuals, of whom this area seems to have had more than its share, wore more elaborate and colorful costumes. Not the least of these were feather mantles, made by fastening feathers to netting, or cloaks made of muskrat skins.

These Southeastern Indians may have lacked a wide variety of clothing, but they more than made up for it in their lavish use of ornaments. They used nearly everything they could lay their hands on—wood, clay, feathers, pearls, bones, copper, stone and shell. From these materials they turned out quantities of beads, necklaces, pendants, rings, ear ornaments, armbands, legbands and hairpins. Pearls from river mussels or Atlantic Coast bivalves were drilled and made into necklaces for chiefs and nobles. Perhaps the most spectacular ornaments were carved, circular shell or copper gorgets.

Nor did they neglect the body itself. Not only did they paint the skin but both men and women also practiced tattooing. Nearly every part of the body might be covered with intricate geometric and naturalistic designs.

Even the hair received its own special treatment. This varied from tribe to tribe. Most women allowed their hair to grow long, sometimes putting it up into a long roll or braiding it. Creek and Chickasaw men shaved their heads, leaving a crest, or roach, from front to back. Some cropped it close on only one side, leaving the opposite side long. Others shaved the entire top of the head and left a fringe around the edges. Still others wore their hair long. Most men rubbed a mixture of bear grease and red paint into their hair.

Practically every Indian tribe in the Southeast made pottery. These Indians were, in many respects, the best potters in the eastern United States. They made pots, buff, gray or black in color, in many different sizes and styles—bowls, plates, cups, bottles, jars, cooking pots, human and animal vessels, and compound pots. Most of the pots were undecorated, made to serve such everyday needs as cooking and storing food. The rest of the pottery was decorated by polishing, incising, engraving, or painting designs in red, white or black. Decorated pots were probably made for burial offerings or for use in certain religious ceremonies.

Smoking seems to have been nearly as universal among these Indians as it is today. In most of the other areas we shall take a look at, smoking was closely tied in with religion and ceremonies. But here nearly everyone seems to have been addicted to tobacco. At least one would assume that from the great number of pipes that archaeologists have dug up.

These pipes were made in an astonishing variety of shapes. Most were manufactured of pottery, but some were carved from stone. They were usually elbow-shaped and probably had wooden or reed stems. Some were fashioned to show crouching human or animal figures, others to represent human or bird or animal heads.

Many of the implements and utensils of these Southeastern Indians were like those already described for the Northeast. However, bark was not used very much in the south, wood or woven cane taking its place. Bark canoes were occasionally made in some sections, but most canoes were dugouts, hollowed out from large cypress trees.

Wood was carved into mortars and pestles, bowls, ladles, spoons, seats and combs. Cane was woven into boxes, mats, shields and baskets. Bone and shell was also widely used.

From the few descriptions the first Spanish explorers have left us, we know that these Indians were artistically inclined. They used many colors, plain or in designs, on buckskin, woven cloaks, feather garments, wooden articles, mats and baskets.

Five hundred years ago there seems to have been much trading among the Southeastern Woodlands. From the coast, traders brought seashells and dried fish into the interior valleys and mountains and traded them for buckskin, red paint, and arrow canes. They carried mica from North Carolina mines northward to the Great Lakes to exchange for chunks of native copper. Flint and salt also had their district sales representatives. From the distant Rocky Mountains they even traded for grizzly-bear teeth. These salesmen established regular trade routes crisscrossing the region. Many of these are now modern four-lane highways.

These Southeastern Indians believed in organization. They had to be organized or they could never have managed to build such huge mounds. The big mound at Cahokia, in East St. Louis, for example, is estimated to have taken one thousand men nearly five years to erect. To accomplish this the Indians put together one of the most complex social and political organizations north of Mexico.

The Creeks and most other Southeastern tribes counted descent through the mother. Each tribe was divided into a number of clans tracing their ancestry through the female line. Each clan was named after some bird or animal— Alligator, Otter, Water Moccasin, Bear, Fox, Wildcat, Skunk, Buzzard.

After marriage, a couple set up housekeeping in the wife's village. To avoid friction, the husband could not speak to his mother-in-law and, in some tribes, could not even see her.

This was one of the few areas in Indian North America where everyone wasn't necessarily born equal. Among many tribes, chiefs, war leaders, priests, nobles and other individuals formed what might be called an aristocracy, or blue-blood society.

In most tribes, chiefs had a great deal of authority. They headed the tribal council and, in some cases, even were seated on stools raised higher than those of the other council members. They were allowed to take more than one wife, had special clothing or marks to show their rank, were carried around in litters and were often protected from the sun by sunshades held by servants. Some chiefs even demanded and received tribute from their subjects.

Each tribe had its war leader, who served as chief of police in time of peace. In addition, he also supervised the ceremonial games.

This feeling of upper-crust society reached a high point among two closely related tribes of the lower Mississippi, the Natchez and the Taensa. Now extinct, the Natchez and the Taensa formerly numbered nearly five thousand people. They lived in eight or ten towns in the vicinity of what is now Natchez, Mississippi.

The Natchez had a class system, with two major divisions of rank, aristocrats and commoners. The aristocratic group was again divided into three classes—Suns, Nobles and Honored People. Commoners were called Stinkards. All the members of the aristocratic group had to marry commoners, while commoners, if they couldn't marry aristocrats, had to settle for commoners. The children of aristocratic women inherited the rank of their mother. Children of common women married to aristocratic fathers fell one grade below the rank of their father. A common man might raise his rank through feats in war, but only to the lowest grade of aristocrats.

The chief of the tribe was called the Great Sun and was believed to be descended from the sun itself. He was treated like an absolute monarch, with a great deal of court etiquette and even court language. When the Sun died, he received a spectacular funeral. His wives and attendants were ceremonially strangled with bowstrings so they could accompany him into the land of the spirits. This was considered a great honor.

Some Southeastern tribes joined together into confederacies. This was a rather loose union of several related tribes banded together for mutual protection against their enemies. Outstanding among such confederacies were those of the Creeks, Choctaws and Cherokees. Within a confederacy, two or three of the larger and more important towns tended to dominate the group, with special council houses where delegates were seated according to rank.

Warfare was the major sport of most Southeastern tribes. The road to success in life was war. Through war a man could attain prestige and personal glory. Through war he gained a new name, earned the right to wear certain paints and feathers and could tattoo the records of his deeds on his body. As a result, most tribes lived in an almost constant state of war with one or another of their neighbors.

Weapons were the usual bows and arrows, darts or spears, bone, stone or reed knives, and clubs. Some clubs might have the knobs spiked with sharp pieces of stone or fish teeth for deadlier effect in hand-to-hand fighting. The warriors of some tribes used wickerwork or bark shields and some even wore wicker armor as well. But most warriors went into battle protected only by their breechcloths, belts, moccasins and elaborate painted designs on their bodies.

Warfare was a time for ceremony. Before a war party set out there was fasting, dancing, body painting, smoking and other rituals. When a successful party returned, there were more ceremonies and celebrations, including the torture of captives. Women and children were often adopted into the tribe. Scalping was practiced, but we don't know how much of it was done before the arrival of the Europeans.

Most Southeastern Indians believed that the earth was flat and the sky a solid vault or shell peopled by sky gods.

Among the Natchez and their neighbors the supreme sky god was the sun. Other tribes revered the sun and also the moon, stars, thunder, lightning and a whole series of lesser spirits. Some believed in giants, elves, demons and ghosts.

Each town had one or more temples perched on top of flat-topped mounds. Some temples held altars; others contained carved wooden images representing the deities.

The Creeks, Natchez, Chickasaws and some other groups had regular staffs of priests to serve the gods. These priests wore distinctive clothing and headdresses and had their own styles of body painting.

Like most farming peoples, these Southeastern Indians held their biggest ceremonies in connection with planting and harvesting their crops. They knew the various seasons of the year, reckoning time by lunar months. The Creeks, along with other tribes, divided the year into two major seasons, winter and summer, as in the following calendar:

WINTER MONTHS

Big Ripening	August
Little Chestnut	September
Big Chestnut	October
Change in Weather	November
Big Winter	December
Little Winter	January

SUMMER MONTHS

Wind Month	February
Little Spring	March
Big Spring	April
Mulberry	May
Blackberry	June
Little Ripening	July

The ripening of the first crops, particularly corn, signaled the end of one year and the beginning of another. The new year's arrival was ushered in by an annual ceremony, the "busk," or green corn ceremony. In preparation for this four- or eight-day celebration the Indians cleaned their houses and themselves and burned their old clothes and other property. Old pots and pans were broken and thrown away. Old fires were put out. A new sacred fire in the temple was lighted by friction and from it new fires were lighted in the houses.

Singing and dancing and the drinking of a sacred black drink were important features of the ceremony. The black drink was an emetic made by boiling the leaves of the holly and certain other plants. This made a strong tea that cleaned out the body and stimulated the mind. It was used in nearly every important ceremony from opening a council meeting to sending off a war party.

After the new fires were lighted, the new green corn was gathered and cooked and eaten at an elaborate feast. At this time the slate was wiped clean and every crime short of murder was forgiven.

Some archaeologists believe a new religious cult arose in the Southeast during the latter part of the Temple Mound period, perhaps just before the Spaniards arrived. They think this because of the many unusual ornaments or ceremonial objects they have dug up in graves and in mounds. These range from pots painted or engraved with skulls, crosses, rattlesnakes and feathered or flying horned serpents, to shell and copper gorgets, breastplates, and stone palettes carved with human trophy heads, weeping-eye symbols, winged rattlesnakes, spiders and other weird figures. Many of these designs seem to have been imported from Mexico. Archaeologists have called this new religious idea the Southern Death Cult, or Buzzard Cult. Whatever it was, it was on the decline when European settlers began pouring into the area.

The Southeastern Indians had their shamans, or medicine men. Most of these were specialists. Some cured disease; others foretold the future. Still others controlled the weather and practiced magic and witchcraft on the side.

Most of these tribes took special care of their dead. There were elaborate mourning ceremonies. Frequently the fire in the house was put out and a new one laid, or the house of the deceased might be burned. Some tribes buried their dead in graves, laying away the bodies full-length or folding or flexing them by bringing the knees up under the chin. In other tribes the bodies of chiefs were dried and placed around the inner wall of their temples. The Choctaw and Natchez and certain other tribes exposed the bodies on scaffolds. Later, the bones were cleaned by "buzzard men" or "bone pickers" and then stored in cane boxes in special bone houses.

The Southeasterners, like most American Indians, were equally interested in the brighter side of life. They were especially fond of games. They had numerous games of chance, played with marked sticks or pebbles.

The favorite game throughout the Southeast, as well as the Northeast, Woodlands was lacrosse. This game, which has today been taken over by Americans and Canadi-

Iroquois lacrosse rackets

ans, was as much a national game to these Indians as
baseball is with us. It originated somewhere in this Woodlands region. The Indians used a stuffed deerskin ball and
wooden rackets with netting of twisted squirrel skin or
Indian hemp fiber.

Lacrosse was a ceremonial as well as a social sport.
Games were played on a ceremonial ball field. Towns or
tribes were often matched against each other. The Indians loved to gamble, and stakes were frequently heavy.

Players might number from a dozen to a hundred or more on either side. Play was rough and broken bones were common.

Another popular game was chunkey, played with a smooth stone disk some six inches in diameter and poles with a crook at one end. The object of the game was to roll the disk along a level court and slide the poles after it. The winner was the one whose pole finally came to rest closest to the stone. This was an extremely old game. Handsomely carved chunkey stones have been found in many archaeological sites.

Today, there are only a handful of Indians living in the Southeastern United States. Many tribes are now extinct. A few Cherokees still live in North Carolina and several hundred Seminoles in the Florida Everglades. The rest, including the remnants of the Five Civilized Tribes, are now in Oklahoma.

5

Desert Dwellers of the Southwest

IN THE summer of 1540, barely twenty years after Cortez had conquered the Aztecs, Francisco Vásquez de Coronado led an army of gold-hungry Spanish adventurers northward into what is now Arizona and New Mexico. Their pockets emptier than when they left home, Coronado and his men finally went back to Mexico, not at all impressed with either the country or its inhabitants.

The famed Seven Cities of Cibola, about which they had heard so many tales, instead of being paved with gold and silver and precious stones had turned out to be merely the homes of the Hopi, Zuñi and Rio Grande Pueblo Indians. The Spaniards had given the Indians their name, Pueblos, the Spanish word for villages or towns, because of their stone and mud community houses. Today we use the term for both the Indians and their houses.

The locale of the amazing Pueblo Indians and their equally surprising neighbors is the Southwest. This is the term anthropologists use for the area covered by the present-day states of Arizona and New Mexico, together with adjoining parts of Colorado, Utah, Nevada, California, Texas and northern Mexico.

In direct contrast to the forested, well-watered Eastern Woodlands, this is dry land, rocky land, an up-and-down land of canyons and mesas, of sandy deserts and tree-rimmed mountains. Above all it is a land of color—of reds and pinks and grays and browns and greens. There is no other region quite like it anywhere in the world.

Given such a setting, you can readily understand why the original inhabitants lived very differently from their distant relatives east of the Mississippi. Actually, when the Spaniards arrived, there were three different groups of Southwestern Indians living three different ways of life.

The Hopi, the Zuñi and other Pueblo Indians lived on the high plateaus of northern Arizona and New Mexico. Along the Arizona-New Mexico boundary and eastward throughout most of New Mexico were half a dozen Apache tribes, including the Navaho. In southern and western Arizona were the Pima, the Papago and various Yuman tribes. Archaeologists estimate that there were a little over 100,000 of these Indians living here in 1540.

Since these Indians lived such diverse ways of life, we can't describe them as we did the people of the Eastern Woodlands but shall have to take each in turn.

Farmers, Weavers and Potters

We shall begin our survey with the Pueblo Indians. They may not be the Southwest's oldest inhabitants, but they can trace their ancestry back for well over two thousand years.

Their homeland is often called the Four Corners coun-

Sandals worn by the prehistoric Anasazi of northeastern Arizona

try, where Arizona, New Mexico, Colorado and Utah meet at right angles. This is the only such place in the United States where four states come together.

Before the beginning of the Christian Era, Indians were living in this Four Corners country in caves or in circular pit structures. Archaeologists named these people Basket Makers because of their many colorful baskets. The Basket Makers borrowed corn and squash from their southern neighbors, the Mogollon people, and began to settle down in permanent pit houses grouped in small villages. Later, they borrowed still more from the south, beginning with pottery and ending up with beans, stone axes and hammers, the bow and arrow, and the hard cradleboard.

The last item doesn't sound like anything one would want to borrow. Yet its use changed the looks of the Basket Makers. It flattened the skulls of its wearers and, within a few generations, made broader and shorter heads out of what had been long and narrow ones. Archaeologists call these new broad-headed people Pueblo. Scientists have still another name for the Basket Makers and Pueblos. They call them the Anasazi, The Ancient Ones, from the Navaho Indian term for builders of these prehistoric ruins.

About A.D. 750 or 800 the Pueblos, now equipped with finer tools, began to build bigger and better houses of stone and mud. By A.D. 1100 they were constructing hundreds of multistoried apartment houses in the caves and out in the valleys. But by 1300 the Pueblo golden age had come to an end. Archaeologists don't know exactly why. Perhaps it was a great drought that hit the Southwest between 1276 and 1299, as a study of tree rings tells us. Perhaps it was invading, warlike nomads. Whatever the reason, the Cliff Dwellers and their Pueblo relatives out in the open towns abandoned the Four Corners country and moved south and east to found new settlements.

By the time Coronado discovered the Southwest, the Pueblo Indian homeland had dwindled to three centers—the Hopi in northeastern Arizona, the Zuñi in western New Mexico, and the Rio Grande in north-central New Mexico. Of all the hundreds and hundreds of cliff dwellings and pueblos built and lived in during the preceding centuries, there were only some seventy left.

After Coronado departed for Mexico in 1542, the Pueblo Indians were left more or less alone until 1598, when the Spaniards came back to stay. In 1680 the Pueblos, united for the only time in their history, rose up against their conquerors and drove them southward to what is now El Paso, Texas. But the Pueblos couldn't remain united, and twelve years later the Spaniards reconquered them without firing a shot.

By 1700, through a combination of disease, Spaniards and war, the seventy-odd pueblos had been reduced to some twenty-five or thirty. But that is history. We shall retrace our steps a hundred years and see how the Pueblo Indians lived before the Spaniards moved in with them.

In the first place, the Pueblo Indians were not all alike. They did not form a single tribe with a single language. Each town was separate from the others, often with its own language. The Hopi, the Zuñi, and nearly two-thirds of the Rio Grande Pueblos belonged to the Aztec-Tanoan language family. But most of them couldn't understand one another. The Hopi and Zuñi were distinct languages, while the Rio Grande Pueblos spoke one or another of three or four different Tanoan languages. The other half-dozen or so Rio Grande Pueblos spoke a Keresan language that may be distantly related to the Siouan family.

The Pueblo Indians may have differed among themselves in their language, but they all shared about the same way of life. Before Columbus, the Pueblo and their southern neighbors, the Hohokam, were the only real farmers in the United States. To the Eastern Woodlands Indians, farming was generally secondary to hunting, fishing and gathering. But to the Pueblos it was the basis of their existence.

Despite the dry, often sandy, country, the Pueblo farmers raised crops of corn, beans, squash, gourds, tobacco and even cotton. According to many experts, they were the world's finest dry farmers, taking advantage of every drop of the scanty seasonal rainfall. To look at a Hopi cornfield today, with the stalks barely three feet high, you wouldn't think very much of it. Yet it yields excellent, heavy ears.

To us, most corn is either yellow or white. But the Pueblo Indians grew corn in all colors—yellow, white, black, blue, pink and even speckled. And they did all their planting and cultivating by hand, with wooden digging sticks and wooden-handled stone hoes.

In contrast to the East, where women were the farmers, here men did most of the farming, with the women helping out only during planting and harvesting times.

The Pueblo Indians didn't pass up hunting entirely. Some of the eastern Pueblos went out to the plains and brought back bison or buffalo. The others had to be satisfied with deer, antelope and, particularly, rabbits. There wasn't enough water around for them to worry about trying to catch fish. Meanwhile, the women gathered wild berries and piñon nuts.

Lacking the East's bark, timber and grass with which to build their houses, the Pueblo Indians were forced to

Taos Pueblo, New Mexico

Courtesy, Bureau of American Ethnology, Smithsonian Institution
Pueblo of Zuñi, New Mexico, in 1879

use the things they had in greatest abundance—stone and mud. Out of stone or adobe, they built rectangular, flat-roofed rooms placed side by side to form a solid block like an apartment house. These were from one to four or five stories high, the upper floors set back in terraces like a skyscraper. Some of these houses were constructed around the sides of an open courtyard or plaza. Others were arranged in rows along what might be termed streets.

These were the biggest Indian cities put up north of

Zuñi Indian woman making pottery

Zuñi Indian woman carrying water

Mexico. Some of the prehistoric towns, like Pueblo Bonito in New Mexico, stood four stories high and contained over eight hundred rooms. But in historic times they were slightly smaller. Today, Taos and Zuñi are the skyscrapers of the Pueblo world, each reaching five stories in height.

Most walls were plastered inside and out with a coating of fine clay like whitewash. Rooms on the bottom floor often lacked outside doorways, perhaps for better protection against enemies. They were entered by notched log ladders through a hatchway in the roof. Upper-floor rooms might have either small side doorways or roof hatchways. Since the rooms were usually on the dark side, the people carried on most of their work on the terraced roofs in front of their apartments or in the plaza below.

Houses were furnished with a stone or clay-lined fireplace, rush or willow mats, tanned deerskins, a stone storage bin or two, and perhaps a pole shelf. One of the most important pieces of household furniture was the metate. This Aztec word means a corn grinding stone. On this slightly concave stone slab dried corn could be ground into meal by rubbing with a smaller stone called a mano, the Spanish word for hand.

Pots and pans also occupied a prominent place in every well-run household. The Pueblo Indians were the best potters north of Mexico. They manufactured utensils in all sizes and shapes—bowls, platters, ladles, mugs, pitchers, canteens, cooking vessels and storage jars. They even put handles on many of their pots. Many were decorated with elaborate designs in black, white, red, yellow, orange, pur-

Prehistoric Pueblo black-on-white pottery

ple or green paint. Each town or group of towns had its own distinctive style of decoration.

We don't have the space to describe all the things these energetic people made. They were excellent craftsmen, turning out everthing from stone axes to clay pipes to bone needles. They spun cotton into thread and wove it into cloth. Curiously, the men were the chief weavers. Women made fine baskets, often decorating them in color.

They used cotton for much of their clothing, weaving it into breechcloths, poncho-type shirts, belts, aprons and skirts. From yucca and other wild plant fibers they wove bands and aprons and sandals to fit every member of the family. For cold weather they wore robes woven of turkey feathers or rabbit fur. They loved ornaments, particularly turquoise. But they also made beads, pendants and necklaces of stone and shell.

The Pueblo Indians were great traders. The Hopi traded their surplus cotton cloth to the Rio Grande Indians. They obtained shells from as far away as the Gulf of California and the Pacific Coast. From northern Mexico they imported bright-colored parrot and macaw feathers, sending back turquoise in trade.

Compared to the Eastern Woodlands Indians, the Hopi and the Zuñi and other Pueblo Indians were peaceful. Almost the only time they ever fought was when nomadic raiders tried to rob them of their stores of corn and beans. The name Hopi means "peaceful people."

Each town had its own village chief and council of elders and often a war chief. But the latter served primarily for defensive warfare. Each town also had its clans, with descent traced on the mother's side of the family. Clans had such names as Wood, Reed, Flute, Snake, Rabbit, Ant, Eagle and Hawk.

Religion to the Pueblo Indians was not a take-it-or-leave-it affair. Their entire life revolved around religion. Most Pueblo men spent nearly half their time engaged in some form of religious or ceremonial activity. Cutting across the clan system, for example, were secret societies—Kachina societies, curing or medicine societies, and warrior societies. These had their social as well as their religious side. A man might belong to all three organizations.

Like the Southeasterners, the Pueblos had their separate ceremonial houses, usually partly underground,

Curing ceremony in kiva at Zia Pueblo, New Mexico

called kivas. These served as ceremonial centers and also as clubhouses or workrooms for the men.

Most of the Pueblos had an elaborate series of ceremonies performed at fixed times during the year. Rituals were generally put on to bring rain or to insure abundant crops. Many of the ceremonies involved the kachinas, the spirits of supernatural beings, who were impersonated in masked dances. Some ceremonies began with secret rites in the kiva, followed by a public performance in the plaza. Smoking was an important feature of most ceremonies, often beginning and ending them.

Each group had its special ceremonies. The Hopi are

Hopi Snake Dance at Mishongnovi Pueblo, 1885

world-famous for their Snake Dance, still given each year
in August to bring rain to their crops. This is a nine-day
ceremony. During the first four days the priests go out in
each of the four directions to gather live snakes, preferably
rattlesnakes, though other varieties are also collected.
After further secret rites in the kiva, the ceremony ends
on the ninth day with a public dance in the plaza. Priests
hold the live snakes in their mouths and carry them
around the courtyard. At the close of the ceremony, the
snakes are set free in all four directions from the pueblo.
The snakes, being thought of as sacred messengers of the
gods, then supposedly tell the gods to bring rain. It might

be added that rain generally does fall before the sun goes down.

The other Pueblos also have their colorful ceremonies, many of which are open to the public. The Zuñi have their Shalako ceremony in December, the Rio Grande Pueblos their Corn Dances.

The Pueblo Indians are conservatives. Today, even after four hundred years of exposure to Spanish, Mexican and American civilization, the Pueblo way of life has changed relatively little.

Farmers of the Arizona Deserts

South and west of the Pueblos, in southern and western Arizona, lay the second major cultural division in the Southwest. This was home for the Pima and related Papago Indians of southern Arizona and half a dozen Yuman-speaking tribes scattered up and down the Colorado River.

This is hotter and drier country than the northern plateaus of the Pueblos. It is a land of sand and cactus and greasewood, the abode of lizards and rattlesnakes and roadrunners. It is not the kind of country you would expect primitive farmers to pick to settle down in and build towns.

Yet farmers had settled here well before the opening of the Christian Era. Archaeologists call these people the Hohokam, a Pima Indian word for "the people who have gone." The Hohokam Indians seem to have been the descendants of the earlier Cochise seed-gatherers of southeastern Arizona and southwestern New Mexico. When they acquired corn and pottery from Mexico, they moved into the Gila and Salt river valleys in southern Arizona.

During the following centuries they borrowed beans and squash to add to their menus and cotton to be woven into cloth. But their greatest discovery was in learning how to dig irrigation ditches that would bring water from the rivers to water their fields. Without these ditches their crops would have dried up. By A.D. 1100 or 1200 hundreds of miles of these irrigation canals crisscrossed the valley in and around what is now Phoenix, Arizona. Some of these ditches were huge, measuring thirty feet wide and seven feet deep. Dug out with wooden digging sticks and stone hoes, with the dirt carried off in baskets, they were not easy to build. A few of these ancient canals have been cleaned out and are now in use as part of modern irrigation systems.

The Hohokam lived in large pit houses, rectangular or oblong in shape, with the floors below the surface of the ground from a few inches to a foot or two. The walls and roof were formed of a framework of poles and reeds and grass plastered over with a thick layer of dirt. A covered entrance passage sloped upward to ground level. With a fireplace in the center and a smoke hole in the roof, such houses were warm in winter and relatively cool in summer. These single-room houses were grouped in small villages along the Gila and Salt rivers and down the Santa Cruz valley to Tucson. Some were even located out in the desert at the end of long canals.

These desert dwellers were noted for their distinctive pottery, buff-colored with designs in red paint, their fine stone and shell carvings, and for their unusual habit of cremating their dead and placing the ashes and charred bones in large pottery jars. From far down in Mexico they had also imported a ceremonial ball game. Archaeologists have found and excavated a number of the large courts on which the game was played. At one late site they even uncovered a rubber ball which had probably been used in the game.

During the thirteenth and fourteenth centuries, the Salado people, a mixture of Anasazi and Mogollon groups, moved from the southern fringes of the plateaus into Hohokam territory. This was a peaceful invasion. The newcomers made themselves right at home and seemed to have lived happily side by side with their hosts.

They taught the desert dwellers how to build houses out of mud. These were thick-walled houses of adobe clay put up side by side like the northern apartment houses. But most of them were only one or two stories high. The dozen or more houses forming the village were usually enclosed within a massive adobe wall.

A few of these Salado houses were three and four stories in height. One at Los Muertos contained thirty-six community buildings and a great many small houses. One of the most famous of these sites is preserved today at Casa Grande National Monument, near Coolidge, Arizona. At Casa Grande (meaning "big house") there was one huge four-story house and a number of smaller structures surrounded by a great wall four feet thick and perhaps seven feet high.

The Salado people enlarged the irrigation system to take care of the increased population. They brought in their own pots and pans, decorated in colorful black and white and red paints. They also brought in their northern practice of burying their dead in graves in the ground.

Yet most of the Hohokam people continued to cremate their dead. They continued to make their own red-on-buff pottery. And some conservatives continued to build and live in shallow pit houses.

About A.D. 1400, the Salado Indians packed up their bags and departed eastward. Why they left, we don't know. Nor do we know exactly where they went. Some archaeologists think they may have joined forces with some of their Pueblo relatives in New Mexico. Others believe at least a part may have gone into Chihuahua, Mexico.

So far as we know, the Hohokam people stayed right where they had been for centuries. But they let the adobe houses and walls fall into ruins and returned to living in shallow pit houses clustered together in small villages.

In the meantime other Hohokam Indians had been living south of the Gila and Salt rivers in southwestern Arizona. This was pure desert country. Without permanent streams to tap for irrigation canals, these Indians had to be content with smaller fields irrigated only by flood waters and occasional rains. Yet, by hunting and by gathering mesquite beans and the fruit of various cactus plants they were able to make a fair living. They differed from their river relatives in their limited use of stone and shell carving, in making red-on-brown instead of red-on-buff pottery, and in their custom of burying their dead rather than cremating them.

The Salado invaders didn't get down into this desert country. It may have been too barren and too dry for their taste. Or the series of forts and fortified outposts the desert Indians built along the rocky ridges overlooking the valleys may have helped put a stop to any ideas the Salado people might have had about pushing on southward.

We don't know too much about these river and desert Hohokam Indians during the next couple of centuries after the Salado people pulled up stakes. The Spanish explorers of 1539 and 1540 seem to have bypassed this region, keeping to the higher and cooler mountains to the east. Later Spanish explorers and settlers heading for New Mexico and northern Arizona also detoured around this hot, dry desert country.

When the first Spanish missionaries finally did appear in southern Arizona in the late 1600's, they found the Pima and Papago Indians occupying the river and desert territory formerly inhabited by the Hohokam people. Since these seventeenth-century Indians were also living much the same kind of life as the earlier Hohokam, most archaeologists look on the Pimas and Papagos as the direct descendants of the prehistoric Indians.

Except for slight local variations, Papago and Pima Indians speak the same language.

Both lived in circular, dome-shaped houses of poles and

brush covered with earth, with a low, rectangular opening left in the side for the doorway.

The Pimas were primarily farmers, depending upon their irrigated fields of corn, beans and squash. The Papagos, whose name means The Bean People, raised the same crops. But they had to rely for nearly half their food on what they could hunt and gather. The men hunted deer, antelope, jackrabbits, mountain sheep, pack rats and an occasional quail or dove. The women gathered mesquite beans, plant seeds, wild potato roots, the buds and fruits of several varieties of cacti and, particularly, the fruits of the giant cactus. Since this last plant often grew to a height of twenty-five feet or more, the fruit had to be gathered with a long, slender pole.

The Pimas also raised a great deal of cotton which they wove into cloth. Most of the Papagos got their cotton by trade with the Pimas.

Living in a warm, often hot, country, neither of these tribes needed to wear much clothing. Women wore a one-piece wraparound skirt of cotton or buckskin reaching from the waist to the knees. Men wore only a breechcloth of buckskin or cotton cloth. Both men and women protected their feet against cactus and other thorns with yucca fiber sandals. For cold weather they used robes of cotton cloth or of rabbit fur.

Most people left their hair long and flowing. On special occasions they painted their bodies red, yellow and white. Every adult woman also had her face tattooed with blue lines running from the corners of her mouth to the chin.

Some desert trees, like mesquite and ironwood, produced tough and durable wood. From these the Indians made many of their implements and utensils. The two chief arts of the women were pottery-making and basketry.

Unlike the Pueblos, the Pima clan organization was weak. Descent was traced through the father. The village, with its head chief, seems to have played the most important part in the life of the people. Medicine men were prominent in both tribes. But dances and ceremonies were not as frequent or as elaborate as those of the Pueblo peoples.

All along the Colorado River, from the Gulf of California to the Grand Canyon, lived another prehistoric people. Archaeologists call this culture the Patayan, named after a Walapai Indian word meaning "the old people."

So far archaeologists haven't been able to find out too much about these Patayan people. They seem to have lived in brush huts. They farmed in the flood plains along the river, raising the usual corn, beans and squash. They made brownish-colored pottery, occasionally decorating it with red designs. In some areas they cremated their dead; in others they buried them.

The Patayan people were probably the ancestors of the Indians the Spaniards found occupying the valley in the sixteenth and seventeenth centuries. There were seven of these tribes, all speaking closely related Yuman languages. Along the lower river were the Cocopa, Maricopa and Yuma tribes. Northward, around Needles, lived the Mohave Indians. Further up the Colorado were the Walapai, with the Havasupai living in Cataract Canyon just

Courtesy, Bureau of American Ethnology, Smithsonian Institution

Pima Indian woman grinding corn on a metate

south of the Grand Canyon. The last group, the Yavapai, were located around Prescott, Arizona.

Physically, these were tall Indians, the tallest in the Southwest and one of the tallest groups in the United States.

Farming was not too important among most of these tribes, taking a backseat to hunting, gathering and fishing. They built brush- or dirt-covered houses like those of the Pimas. On account of the warm climate, the Indians needed very little clothing. About all that they wore were skin breechcloths for the men and bark aprons for the women. Both men and women were often elaborately tattooed.

The Yuman peoples were not too skilled in arts and crafts. Most of them did, however, make pottery and basketry, some of which was fairly good.

They had few ceremonies, but organized religious ceremonies were not important to them. Dreams were the foundation for almost everything in life from success in war or marriage to becoming a shaman.

Death was one of the few occasions when there was much ceremony or ritual. The Yuman tribe cremated their dead, laying the body on a huge pile of driftwood logs and setting fire to it. This was a public ceremony, involving singing, dancing, fasting and speechmaking.

War was a sport to the Yumas and Mohaves and some of the other tribes. Fighting was often formal, with challenges and speeches and duels before the battle became general. The Yumas liked to fight with a special wooden club shaped like a potato masher.

Nomadic Raiders of the Southwest

The half dozen Apache tribes, including their close relatives, the Navaho, form the third great division of Southwestern Indians. Unlike the other two groups, the Apache tribes were newcomers to the area, not old settlers.

All of the Apache tribes speak closely allied Athabascan languages. Their nearest relatives are far to the north in Canada. Most anthropologists think the Apaches broke off from their Canadian relatives about a thousand years ago and migrated southward, landing in the Southwest in the sixteenth century, not too long before the Spaniards arrived from the south.

We can forget about two of the Apache tribes, the Lipan and Kiowa-Apache, as they lived out on the plains to the east. Of the other five groups, the Jicarilla Apaches ranged over northeastern New Mexico and southeastern Colorado, the Mescalero Apaches southcentral New Mexico and southwestern Texas. Down in southeastern Arizona, southwestern New Mexico, and northern Mexico lived the Chiricahua Apaches, with the Western Apaches in eastern Arizona and the Navaho in northeastern Arizona and northwestern New Mexico.

Everyone has heard or read stories about the Apache Indians. The chances are excellent that not all you have heard or read is true. The Apaches have generally been called fighters, raiders and killers. They have been labeled bloodthirsty murderers, cruel, ruthless and inhuman. At one time or another some Apaches were all of these.

But they were also potters and basket-makers and farmers and deeply religious family men. This is a side of their life that not many know about. While the Apaches were far from being angelic, they were not the inhuman savages that they have so often been pictured.

When the Apaches first hit the Southwest, they were probably nomads, hunting and gathering for their living. Most of them soon picked up farming from their Pueblo neighbors and raised small crops of corn, beans and squash. Yet they continued to hunt and gather for the major part of their food supply.

We don't know how soon they began to raid the Pueblos and the Spanish and Mexican settlements. But it couldn't have been too long. Not all the fault lay on their side. The Spanish and Mexican colonists pouring into New Mexico began crowding the Apaches out of the fertile river valleys. To cap it all, many Spaniards looked on the Apaches as a handy and cheap source of slave labor to work their mines and fields. The Apaches returned the favor by raiding and killing. Moreover, many Spaniards and Mexicans secretly encouraged Apache raiding. What was picked up by the Apaches in one town found a quick buyer in another town several hundred miles away.

Once they began raiding, they couldn't stop. It became a business with them. Without the loot captured in raids many Apaches would have starved to death.

With the exception of the Navaho, who lived in earth-covered hogans, the other Apaches lived in wickiups. These were circular, conical or dome-shaped houses built over a framework of poles and brush and thatched with

Courtesy, Bureau of American Ethnology, Smithsonian Institution

Navaho summer hut, Keams Canyon, Arizona

bear grass. In winter or in rainy weather the wickiup was covered with skins.

Apache clothing was made almost entirely of deerskin. The men wore breechcloths and buckskin shirts and thigh-high moccasins. The women wore two-piece dresses of buckskin and high-topped moccasins. Both men and women generally left their hair long. To keep the loose hair out of his eyes the Apache man tied a strip of buckskin around his head.

The Apaches were not feathered Indians. Some of the Jicarilla and Mescalero Apaches, who lived next door to the Plains Indians, adopted warbonnets. But the rest of the Apaches didn't ordinarily wear feathers in their hair.

Both men and women were fond of wearing ornaments, particularly turquoise and abalone shell. These were, however, worn more as religious or protective amulets than as ornaments. Neither men nor women went in for face or body painting.

Moving around as much as they did, the Apaches couldn't afford to load themselves down with many household implements and utensils. About all they had were baskets of several different sizes and shapes, an occasional clay pot, perhaps a few cups or dishes made of gourds, skin bags, stone metates and manos, bone awls, a wooden fire drill, and a baby cradleboard.

Only the Navaho and Western Apaches had clans, with descent traced through the mother. But the principal social and economic unit in most tribes was the extended family. It was made up of an elderly couple, their unmarried sons and daughters, and their married daughters and their

Three Navaho Indian
chiefs in 1874

husbands. The married sons weren't included because, when a man got married, he had to make his home with his wife's people. This was hard on the man because, to show his respect, he had to avoid his mother-in-law. He could not look at her, be in the same house with her or even speak directly to her. This was often difficult and has given rise to a lot of Apache mother-in-law jokes.

Most of the Apache tribes had no formal tribal government. The most common governing body in a tribe was the local group or band, made up of several of these extended families, headed by a chief. The local group chief was generally more of an adviser than an absolute ruler. When a number of local groups got together to organize a raid or war party, the most influential of the local group chiefs headed the combined band.

The Apaches were extremely religious, believing in a host of supernatural beings. They had ceremonies for almost everything from finding lost objects to curing sick people. One of the most colorful and dramatic Apache ceremonies was the coming-out ceremony for girls, its highlight being the appearance of masked dancers. Medicine men, or shamans, were important figures in Apache society, their supernatural power aiding them in curing disease.

Warfare also had its ceremony. Medicine men with war powers generally accompanied the warriors. It is astonishing how successful Apache war parties were, considering how few in number the warriors were. The usual war party consisted of from a dozen to fifty or sixty fighting men. Probably only once or twice in the entire history of the Southwest did several hundred Apache warriors ever get together at one time. Actually, war parties had to be small because most Apache tribes were also small.

The Navaho numbered less than fifteen thousand as late as 1860. The two tribes that caused more trouble than any others, the Chiricahua and Western Apache, together added up to a bare five thousand people, including men, women and children.

Yet this handful of Indians, armed with bows and arrows, spears, clubs and knives, kept the Southwest on its toes for two hundred years. Army officers who should have known what they were talking about called the

Apache Indian woman with baby in cradleboard

Navaho Indian warrior with lance and shield

Chiricahua and Western Apaches the greatest all-around fighters of all American Indians.

Today, in marked contrast to most other culture areas in North America north of Mexico, there are more Indians living in the Southwest than there were in the sixteenth century.

Another unique feature about this area is that most of the Indians still live in much the same places as their ancestors did when they were discovered over four hundred years ago.

6

Hunters and Farmers of the Plains

TO MOST of us the horseback-riding, buffalo-hunting, warbonneted Indian of the Plains represents the real American Indian. This is the Indian of fiction and motion pictures and popular fancy. Yet what is not generally known is that this picture of the Plains Indian is only a century or two old. It came into being long after the discovery of the New World.

The Plains area was the largest cultural area in North America north of Mexico. It extended all the way from southern Canada to Texas and from the Mississippi River westward to the Rocky Mountains. Treeless except for the river valleys, this was open, rolling grasslands, broken only by a few scattered hills. The Missouri River and its hundreds of tributary streams furnished an abundance of water.

This was buffalo country, the home of millions of buffalo, or bison. The hills and valleys literally teemed with other game—mountain sheep, deer, elk, antelope, grizzly bear, beaver and all kinds of waterfowl.

These river valleys and grasslands were also home for some twenty different Indian tribes speaking languages belonging to five different families, as shown in the following chart:

Plains Language Families and Major Tribes

ALGONKIAN FAMILY

Arapaho	Gros Ventre
Blackfoot	Piegan
Blood	Plains Cree
Cheyenne	

ATHABASCAN FAMILY

Kiowa-Apache	Sarsi

AZTEC-TANOAN FAMILY

Comanche	Kiowa

CADDOAN FAMILY

Arikara	Wichita
Pawnee	

SIOUAN FAMILY

Assiniboine	Mandan
Crow	Omaha
Dakota (Sioux)	Osage
Hidatsa	Oto
Iowa	Ponca
Kansa	

Although some closely related groups within the same language family could understand each other—for instance, the Piegan, Blood and Blackfoot or the Pawnee and Arikara—most of the others could not. To overcome this language barrier and to make trading easier, the

Plains Indians invented an extremely effective sign language. By signs and gestures made with the fingers and hands, they learned to communicate with one another as fluently as we do by oral speech. To illustrate the system, the right hand held out, palm down, with only the first two fingers extended, meant "I see." Both hands held up shoulder high, with the fingers pointing upward, meant "an elk."

Through sign language a Siouan-speaking Dakota Indian could exchange ideas and information with an Algonkian-speaking Cheyenne or an Aztec-Tanoan-speaking Comanche. So effective was this sign language that the Indians could talk for hours on end without a single word being spoken.

Anthropologists estimate that there were slightly more than 100,000 Indians living in the Plains area at the beginning of the sixteenth century. The Dakota or Sioux, with its seven tribal divisions, was the largest single group. Other large Plains tribes were the Pawnee, Assiniboine, Comanche, Osage, Crow, Arikara, Mandan and Cheyenne.

Thousands of years before these Indian tribes roamed the Plains, other early Americans had discovered this hunter's paradise. First, some 10,000 to 15,000 years ago, came the elephant hunters, their chief target the mighty mammoth or mastodon. When these animals disappeared from the region, the hunters turned their stone-tipped spears on a smaller but more abundant game animal, the giant bison. Campsites of these bison hunters have been found along the high plains from Canada southward to Texas and New Mexico.

A few thousand years later the Ice Age ended. With it came the extinction of most of the animals men had hunted—mammoth and mastodon, giant bison, horse, camel and ground sloth. The present-day type of bison, or buffalo, smaller in size than its predecessor but still big enough to furnish meat for a large banquet, managed to survive.

Even though some of the big-game hunters were turning more and more to gathering wild plants for a living, many still continued to hunt buffalo. Shortly before the beginning of the Christian Era, pottery from the Eastern Woodlands began to make its way to the Plains. Not too many centuries later corn and beans and squash followed.

Within another few centuries small villages of square or rectangular houses covered with earth dotted the valleys of the eastern Plains. These were pit houses, dug down into the ground from two to four or five feet so that they would be warm in winter and cool in summer. Some villages were protected by encircling ditches and post stockades. These farmers also must have been buffalo hunters because their major cultivating implement was a hoe made from the shoulder blade of a bison.

By the time Columbus arrived in America, these villages had become fewer in number but larger in size. They were concentrated along the larger rivers. Houses were now circular in form, built of poles and willow branches laid over a framework of heavy timbers and covered with grass and then with a thick layer of dirt. Some of these earth lodges were huge, measuring fifty to sixty feet in diameter, but most ranged from twenty to forty feet. The largest of these could accommodate forty or more people and, in later days, even a horse or two. Long, tunnel-like, covered entrances led to the interiors of these dome-shaped houses. Skin curtains were hung at the inner and outer ends to keep out the cold. There was a fireplace in the center and an opening in the roof for a smoke hole. Couches were built around the sides. Covered with buffalo robes, they served as seats by day and beds by night.

Courtesy, American Museum of Natural History

Model of Mandan skin-covered bullboat

Surrounding the thirty to fifty or more closely grouped earth lodges that comprised the average town was an eight- to ten-foot-deep ditch. On the village side of the ditch a high stockade of logs provided additional protection.

These town dwellers were farmers, raising corn, beans and squash. Women did the cultivating, using the shoulder blades of bison as hoes. They stored their surplus farm products in huge, bell-shaped underground storage pits, dug either beneath the floors of their houses or out in the open between houses. These pits were so deep, eight feet or more, that they had to be entered by ladders. At the top they were from two to three feet wide.

Photo by the author

Reconstructed earth lodges, North Dakota

To these settled village dwellers buffalo hunting was secondary. Once or twice a year they would go out on an organized hunt to bring back meat and hides.

The women were also potters, turning out an abundance of clay cooking vessels and storage jars. These were often decorated with simple stamped or incised designs.

Even though these Indians lived on the banks of the Missouri and other large rivers, the only boat they had was a clumsy bullboat, a circular framework covered with buffalo hide.

By the sixteenth and seventeenth centuries we can begin to put names to these valley residents. In North and South Dakota, along the Missouri River, these villages were the homes of the Arikara, Mandan and Hidatsa tribes. Southward, in Nebraska, in and around the Platte River valley, lived the Pawnees. Further south and east lived the other Plains farming tribes, the Iowa, Omaha, Kansa, Osage, Oto, Ponca and Wichita.

Not all the Plains Indians were village dwellers. Only about one-third of them lived in earth lodges in towns along the rivers. The rest of the Plains Indians were nomadic hunters and gatherers, occupying the central and western grasslands where there wasn't enough rainfall to grow crops.

This was the land of such tribes as the Crow, Arapaho, Kiowa, Cheyenne, Blackfoot, Comanche and Dakota. The ancestors of some of these tribes had been living in this grasslands country for a long time. But others were newcomers.

The Crows, for example, were originally North Dakota

Kiowa Indian in 1894 style of dress

Wolf Robe, a Southern Cheyenne Indian

farmers. Along in the seventeenth century, or perhaps a little earlier, they had split off from their relatives, the Hidatsa, and moved west to Montana to hunt buffalo.

As late as the middle of the eighteenth century, the Cheyenne Indians were also still in North Dakota. Here they were farmers and potters, living in earth lodge villages along the river valleys. Yet fifty years later they were out on the plains of Wyoming, Nebraska and Colorado chasing buffalo.

Other latecomers to the Plains were the Dakotas. Although these Indians are and have been popularly known as the Sioux, their own name for themselves is Dakota, meaning friends or allies. There were seven divisions of the Dakota, the largest of which was the Teton-Dakota.

Most of the Dakota were living in Minnesota when they were discovered in the late 1600's. Pressure forced them out of the woodlands into the plains. This pressure started a thousand miles to the east where incoming European settlers were crowding out the coastal tribes. These in turn exerted pressure against their neighbors farther to the west, finally reaching the Dakota. Many Dakota, particularly the Teton, settled in and around the Black Hills of South Dakota. Here, in the nineteenth century, arose such famous Dakota leaders as Crazy Horse, Red Cloud and Sitting Bull.

These western Plains tribes, living a nomadic existence following the buffalo herds, couldn't afford to build the permanent earth lodge of their farming relatives along the

Red Cloud, a Dakota Indian, in feather war bonnet

Missouri River. In its place they evolved the portable, skin-covered tipi (tepee), a Dakota word meaning home or the place where one lives.

The size and method of constructing the tipi varied from tribe to tribe. Some used a three-pole framework, others a four-pole. But everywhere it was the woman's job to put it together. These poles were from fifteen to twenty-five feet long, generally of lodgepole pine with the bark peeled off and the wood rubbed smooth. The three or four poles were laid on the ground and the small ends tied together with rawhide about three feet from the top. They were then raised up and the legs spread to the desired diameter of the tipi, normally ten to twenty feet. Over these, ten to twenty additional similar poles were laid, their tips interlocking with those of the three or four tied poles.

The cover was made of from ten to fifteen dressed buffalo hides carefully fitted and sewn together in one piece. This was lifted up and stretched over the conical framework and pinned together in front with long wooden pins, leaving a low doorway which usually faced the east. This opening was covered by a stiff piece of buffalo hide weighted at the bottom to make it self-closing. The bottom edge of the cover was either staked to the ground or anchored in place with heavy rocks.

To regulate the smoke from the fireplace in the center of the tipi the Plains Indians had worked out a unique arrangement. Attached to the cover at the sides of the smoke hole in the top of the tipi were two flaps, or ears.

To these were tied two long poles. By moving these poles the vent could be operated like a chimney, opening wide or closing in bad weather.

Erecting one of these tipis sounds like a long and complicated job. Yet a couple of women could put one up or take it down in a half hour or less.

The outside of the tipi was sometimes painted with encircling stripes or geometric designs or drawings of buffalo, bear or other animals and birds. An occasional tipi was trimmed with dyed porcupine quills.

The buffalo skin cover of the average tipi weighed from a hundred to a hundred and twenty-five pounds. Hauling these from camp to camp was quite a chore in pre-horse days. The Plains Indians solved the problem by strapping a V-shaped frame of poles, called a travois, to their dogs. Midway toward the dragging butt ends of the two poles a rawhide netting held the load in place. A strong dog could drag a load of fifty to seventy-five pounds. Large tipi covers had to be made in two pieces so they could be carried on two travois. The lodgepoles had to be dragged in the same way.

In dog days, half a dozen miles was a good day's march for a band of Indians moving camp. Sometimes they might not make even that much if some of the dogs took out after a stray rabbit or other animal.

Dog travois were also used by the women to bring in the firewood for the camp and to pack in the meat after a successful buffalo hunt.

The life of these nomadic hunters revolved around the buffalo. The buffalo was their staff of life, furnishing them

Blackfoot Indian dog travois

not only with food but also with the raw materials for their houses, their clothing, their implements and utensils and even their fuel.

Before the introduction of horses and guns, the Indians had to hunt buffalo on foot with bows and arrows and spears. This was hard as well as dangerous work. The Indians used all sorts of tricks to trap animals. A favorite method was to stampede a herd over the edge of a cliff. Archaeologists have found several dozen of these so-called buffalo jumps in Montana and Wyoming alone. Some of these have been used for at least two thousand years. The more elaborate jumps had piles of rocks or lines of stone to help funnel the buffalo to the desired spot at the edge of the cliff. If no cliff was handy, the Indians sometimes set fire to the long prairie grass and drove the animals together so they could more easily be killed. Or animals might be driven into swamps or ponds or man-built traps. In winter, after a heavy snow, buffalo would sink into the drifts and be easy prey for the hunters.

Almost no part of the buffalo was wasted. Hair, skin, meat, blood, entrails, stomach, sinews, bones, horns, hoofs, beard, tail and even the dried dung were all used.

The Indians ate the buffalo's flesh, the marrow of its bones and the brains. Any surplus meat they sun-dried. They had their own K-rations—pemmican. This was made by pounding dried buffalo meat and mixing it with melted fat and marrow and sometimes crushed, dried cherries. It was stored in hide bags or buffalo bladders or intestines and often covered with melted tallow to make it airtight. Sealed in like this, pemmican would keep for years.

Although the lighter and softer deerskin was preferred for clothing, buffalo skins with the hair left on were used as winter robes and winter war moccasins. Buffalo robes also served as bedding and as coverings for backrests. Since green rawhide shrinks when it dries, the Indians used it to bind the heads and handles of axes and hammers and war clubs.

Buffalo hide was fashioned into all kinds of bags, circular shields, ceremonial headdresses and saddles. Distinctive among these hide bags, trunks and cylindrical containers was the parfleche, or expanding bag. This was made of a rectangular piece of rawhide folded so that the long and short sides overlapped. These and all other bags were decorated with geometric designs painted in red, blue, yellow and green.

Buffalo bones were equally useful. Shoulder blades were used by the farmers as hoes and by the other tribes for digging or scraping tools and axes. The ribs were turned into scrapers, arrow straighteners, arrowheads and gaming dice. The leg bones ended up as awls, knives and hammers. Horns were made into spoons, ladles, bowls, cups, powder flasks and headdresses. Skulls served as ceremonial fetishes.

Nor was the stomach overlooked. Cleaned out, it could be used as a water bucket or as a vessel in which to cook stone-boiled soup.

The long, shaggy hair on the buffalo's head and shoulders was braided into rope or woven into bags and belts. Hair was ideal for stuffing rawhide-covered game balls, to cushion beds and to pad saddles. Along with the beard hair, it was made into ornaments for clothing and headdresses. The tail frequently decorated tipis and also had its use as a flyswatter.

Buffalo hoofs might become either rattles or glue. Sinew furnished thread for sewing and cord for bowstrings. Sinew was also used to back bows to increase their springiness. Along with the liver and brains, fat was used to soften and tan hides. Gallstones made excellent yellow paint. Buffalo teeth were pierced and strung on cords as necklaces.

Dried buffalo dung, known as "buffalo chips," was a handy source of fuel when the Indians camped on the treeless plains. The Indians preferred to use chips, as the almost smokeless fire wouldn't betray them to their enemies.

Important as the buffalo was in the life of the Plains Indians, they didn't turn up their noses at deer, elk, antelope, rabbits or other game animals. The women also gathered a great many wild plant foods.

Plains Indian clothing was usually made of soft tanned buckskin. Before the coming of the whites, men wore only moccasins and a small skin apron fastened to a belt. The breechcloth seems to have been a later acquisition. Long skin leggings and shirts were added on special occasions. Women wore full-length sleeveless dresses, moccasins and leggings reaching to the knee. They carried their finer clothes carefully packed away in rawhide wardrobe cases. In contrast to the soft-soled moccasins of the Eastern Woodlands, most Plains moccasins were made in two pieces, with hard rawhide soles.

These Indians loved decoration and frequently painted their clothing or applied geometric designs made of dyed porcupine quills. Some women also decorated their dresses with rows of elk teeth. Once colored beads were introduced by the traders they soon replaced porcupine quills. The Indians sewed rows of beads on nearly every piece of clothing they owned, from belts to moccasins.

Neither men nor women considered themselves well-dressed unless they had on their paint. Red was the favorite color, put on both the face and the upper part of the

Comanche Indian woman in 1872

body. Some individuals tattooed their faces and bodies, but the practice was not universal.

Between 1650 and 1750 the introduction of the horse brought great changes in the ways of Plains Indian life. Horses were first obtained by the southern tribes from the Spanish settlements in New Mexico. But it took nearly a century for the horse to work its way northward to the tribes in Montana and North Dakota.

Not having a word for this new animal, most Plains tribes called it by words meaning "big dog" or "mystery dog."

Once the Plains Indians acquired horses, they became even more nomadic than they had been. They were able to move camp two or three times farther in one day, which allowed them to roam over a much wider territory. They could now accumulate more property and move it farther and faster. A horse could carry two hundred pounds on its back and three hundred on a pole travois.

The horse, in fact, completely revolutionized the economic structure. Up until its coming most Indians in a band or tribe were more or less equal. No one had much more property than his fellow tribesmen. But now a man's wealth was measured in horses. Some had many, others only a few. With an adequate supply of horses, particularly a good hunting horse or two, a man could provide more food, clothing and other things for his family. He could afford a bigger tipi. He could even afford the exchange of gifts necessary to add another wife or two to his household.

The average family needed ten to twelve horses just to carry themselves and their property from one camp to the next. A family with only two or three horses had to be satisfied with a small tipi and few possessions.

The horse made the Plains Indians even more warlike than they had been. Warfare developed into a game where, along with adventure and excitement, a warrior could gain honor and prestige. Like any sport, it followed definite rules and regulations and methods of keeping score.

Killing enemies took second place to the counting of coup. To touch an enemy with the hand or with a special coupstick brought the highest honor. To spear an enemy in hand-to-hand combat was also a high honor. To shoot him at long range with a bow and arrow or gun was a much lesser honor. To most tribes, stealing horses or guns from an enemy was more important than taking scalps.

A man's place in the tribe depended on the war honors he had gained. As a result of his personal achievements he could become a chief. A successful warrior could boast of his exploits and could paint a record of them on the walls of his tipi or on the skin side of a buffalo robe. A man's prestige was also increased by a reputation for generosity. If he stole a dozen horses on a raid, he might give away all but two or three to relatives and friends.

Most wars were small-scale affairs, rarely involving more than a few men eager for glory or loot or revenge. Surprise attack and ambush were characteristic features. The later wars with the settlers, where hundreds and sometimes thousands of Indians fought together, were something new.

Bows and arrows continued to be used long after the introduction of horses and guns. The old-fashioned, single-shot musket was difficult to reload on horseback and could not be fired as rapidly as the bow. In warfare, guns were used more for their sound and shock effects than for their killing ability.

Even in hunting buffalo, the Indian preferred the bow and arrow over the gun. The short bow was well-suited for close-range shooting from horseback. It was powerful enough to send an arrow clear through the body of a buffalo.

Most Plains Indian bows were short, averaging not much more than three feet in length. In the southern grasslands bows were generally made of wood, with osage orange the favorite material. In the north bows were frequently recurved, compound bows made of elk or mountain sheep horn backed with sinew. In early days arrowheads were commonly chipped from flint, although bone and horn arrowheads were also used. But once the Indian began getting triangular iron arrowheads from the traders these quickly replaced the native points.

The feather warbonnet with long flowing tail popularly associated with the Plains Indians was actually not too old. It probably originated among the Siouan tribes and spread from the Dakota to many of the other Plains tribes. The finest headdresses were made of eagle feathers. Warbonnets were not worn by everybody. Only certain men, chiefs and other leaders, were entitled to wear them and then only on special ceremonial occasions or on war parties. Among some tribes one or more eagle feathers were generally worn in the hair by the older and more influential men. Today the warbonnet has become the trademark of the American Indian and is worn by tribes who never even heard of one fifty years ago.

Some Plains Indian tribes had clans with descent traced through the mother; others traced clans through the father; still others had no clans. Most tribes were grouped into a number of loosely organized bands. Each band had its chief, who had little real authority. His job was more that of acting as chairman of an informal council of chiefs. Some were peace chiefs, some war chiefs.

Most tribes also had a number of societies or clubs for men, some of which were ranked according to age. Each fraternity had its officers, its songs, its special paraphernalia. Some were military societies; some were ceremonial;

Courtesy, American Museum of Natural History

Blackfoot man wearing a ceremonial shirt decorated with ermine tails

still others were police societies supervising the buffalo hunt and policing the camp. Typical of such societies were those popularly known as Dog Soldiers.

Plains Indian religion revolved around a belief in impersonal supernatural power. This power was all around, in the sky, in the water, on the land. A man could acquire some of this power through visions while he was fasting in an isolated spot. The man who received such a vision, generally appearing in the form of some animal or bird, would make a medicine bundle of objects associated with that vision. If a man couldn't get a vision of his own, he might buy one from another.

Since nearly everyone had some supernatural power, a medicine man was simply a man who had greater power. Many medicine men were accomplished sleight-of-hand artists, walking on fire or producing animals or plants from inside a person's body.

Some societies or tribes also had larger and more important medicine bundles that were opened only on special ceremonial occasions. Most medicine bundles contained, among other things, tobacco and pipes. The Dakota and some other tribes were famous for their beautifully carved pipes of a red stone called catlinite, or pipestone, which came from a quarry in southwestern Minnesota.

Many Plains tribes had ceremonies to insure success in hunting buffalo. But the most widespread and characteristic ceremony was the Sun Dance. It was the one ceremony that brought all the people in the tribe together. In earlier days the most spectacular feature was self-torture of the dancers. A sharpened wooden stick was run through the victim's skin at the front or back of the chest. To this was fastened a long stout cord, the other end of which was tied to a high pole. Around this he danced until the stick ripped through the flesh.

Most Plains Indians believed it was necessary to purify themselves before taking part in any major ceremony. To do this they built a low, dome-shaped sweat lodge of willow saplings and covered it with skins. Then they heated rocks in a central fireplace. When water was poured on the red-hot rocks, it turned the inside of the nearly airtight hut into a sweat bath.

When an individual died, the body was painted and dressed in its best clothing and wrapped in skin. Frequently it was taken out through the side of the tipi, not through the door. The Indians reasoned that, if the body went out through the regular door, some other occupant of the lodge would soon follow into the spirit world.

Courtesy, Bureau of American Ethnology, Smithsonian Institution
Crow Indian burial scaffold covered with rocks

Among some tribes, the body, along with offerings, was placed in a grave in the ground. Among others it might be put on a burial scaffold on the ground and covered over with rocks. Or the body might be put in the fork of a tree or on a scaffold raised up on four posts. After the body had decomposed, the bones were often laid away in a cave or crevice in the rocks.

The Plains Indian held out as long as he could against the advancing frontier of civilization. But the killing off of the buffalo spelled doom for his way of life and brought an end to one of the most unique and colorful periods in American Indian history.

7

Fishers and Foragers of Streams and Forests

BETWEEN THE Rocky Mountains and the Sierra Nevada and Cascade Mountains of California, Oregon and Washington lies a huge wilderness of deserts and plateaus and mountains. It is a wilderness which extends all the way from British Columbia in Canada southward through western Montana, Idaho, eastern Washington and Oregon, to Nevada and Utah.

In comparison to the other culture areas we have studied so far, this Basin-Plateau area was much more primitive. You can understand why when you take a look at the country. With the exception of parts of the northern plateaus and mountains, it is one of the driest regions in North America.

Cut off by high mountains or broad, sandy deserts from the more advanced tribes of the Plains and the Southwest, the Basin-Plateau Indians never climbed very high on the ladder of civilization. Most of them were too isolated to learn about farming. Even if they did hear about it, their country was either too hot and dry or too cold for corn to grow.

In prehistoric days the inhabitants of this region were hunters and fishers and gatherers. Or so archaeologists tell us, after digging up a score or more caves in which these people used to live. The trash they left behind in Danger Cave, in Fishbone Cave, in Deadman Cave, tells us that these early Indians of 10,000 years ago were scavengers, eating almost anything they could find.

There were few big-game animals in this desert country of Utah, Nevada, southern Idaho and eastern Oregon. But there was an abundance of snakes, lizards, gophers, rats, mice and rabbits. The Indians ate them all. They even caught and ate fish. Archaeologists have uncovered fishnets and fishhooks to prove that there must have been some water in this dry land.

These desert dwellers lived in caves and rock shelters wherever possible, but they also camped out in the open, probably in brush shelters. They used crude manos and metates to grind grass seeds and acorns into meal. They wove baskets and made bags of twisted bark fiber. They seem to have worn skin breechcloths and aprons and fiber sandals, with robes of rabbit fur or bird skins added in cold weather.

In Fort Rock Cave in eastern Oregon archaeologists dug up nearly one hundred square-toed sandals woven of shredded sagebrush bark. Dated by radiocarbon as earlier than 7000 B.C., this cave may well have been the New World's first shoe shop.

North of the Columbia River, the earliest Plateau Indians made more of their living by fishing and hunting than they did by gathering wild seeds and nuts. At least they seem to have found little or no use for the grinding stones so common south of the river. Otherwise, these northerners probably lived much the same way of life as their contemporaries in the southern desert country.

Farming made a brief appearance in southern Utah and southeastern Nevada during the Pueblo era. But once these people moved back to Arizona and New Mexico in the twelfth and thirteenth centuries, corn and beans and the knowledge of how to raise them went right along with them.

The historic period came late for these Basin-Plateau residents. Not until the Lewis and Clark Expedition of 1805–06 did they see their first white man. Yet many of these tribes were already using steel knives and axes, iron arrowheads, glass beads, brass kettles, horses and even a few guns. These had been acquired in trade with some of the Plains Indian tribes.

In the late seventeenth and early eighteenth centuries the Basin-Plateau area, particularly its southern desert section, was not overpopulated. Anthropologists estimate that there were some 64,000 Indians grouped in a great many small tribes. Most tribes spoke languages belonging to one or another of three language families, the Salish, the Sahaptin, and the Aztec-Tanoan (Shoshonean).

Perhaps the best known tribes were the Nez Percé, made famous by Chief Joseph, the Flatheads, the Shoshonis and the Utes and Paiutes. Other tribes included the Thompson River Indians of British Columbia, the

Chief Joseph of the Nez Percé Indians

Shuswap, Okanagon, Umatilla, Wallawalla, Wenatchi, Yakima, Cayuse, Snake, Klickitat, Kalispel, Tenino, and Bannock.

Like their ancestors of 5000 B.C., these Indians were hunters and fishers and gatherers. Lacking agriculture, they had to do the best they could with what nature provided them. Some tribes managed to make a good living while others were not quite so lucky.

Without any question, the most poverty-stricken Indians were those living in the heart of the Great Basin of Nevada and Utah. This was poor country. Rains were few and far between. Both wild plants and animals were scarce. It was hot in summer, cold in winter.

In such a land life wasn't easy for its Shoshonean-speaking inhabitants. They couldn't afford to be choosy about their diet. They had to make the most of everything that walked or crawled or flew or sprouted out of the ground. Big-game animals were few, but jackrabbits were numerous. Several families would often band together to hunt rabbits, driving them into high nets where they could club them to death. Even birds were sometimes caught in nets. The Indians used long sticks with crooks at the end to drag rats and lizards and gophers from their holes.

Every few years great hordes of grasshoppers invaded the area. At such times the Indians had a field day, gathering the grasshoppers in trenches and roasting them alive. Some they feasted on right away; the rest they ground up into flour.

Nuts, wild seeds and roots furnished Basin Indians with much of their living. Piñon nuts, perhaps their most important food, were gathered annually in the mountains. If the harvest was poor, the Indians were in danger of starvation before the end of winter. Their habit of digging for edible roots earned them the name of "Digger Indians" from the whites who passed through the country during the California gold rush.

Their houses were simple pole and brush shelters, often little more than windbreaks. Their clothing was scanty. Men went around naked or wrapped a piece of skin around their waists. Women wore buckskin or cedar bark fiber aprons in front and back. In the camp most Indians went barefoot, putting on skin moccasins or fiber sandals only when they were going on a trip. In cold weather they added a robe of rabbit fur.

Poor though these Basin Indians may have been, some of them were skilled in the art of basketmaking. They made large carrying baskets, trays, seed-beaters, cooking baskets and water jars or canteens covered with pitch to make them watertight. Some of the tribes adjacent to the Southwest, like the Southern Paiute, made pointed-bottom clay pots.

Horses were of little use to these people. Most of them didn't have enough grassland for pasture. They were more likely to kill and eat horses than they were to keep them.

Hunting for food kept the Basin Indians on the move. The scarcity of food also compelled them to live in small bands of a few families each. Such groups needed neither leaders nor government. Several bands might get together only once or twice a year for community antelope hunts.

Under these conditions there was little organized religion or ceremonialism.

They were too busy looking for something to eat to bother about making war on others. Nor did they have enough of anything to make them the target for attacks by neighboring tribes.

The eastern and northeastern Basin tribes, the Utes and Wind River Shoshonis, were much better off than their western relatives. Their Wyoming and Colorado homeland was higher and better watered and had an abundance of game and wild plant foods.

They were close enough to the Plains tribes to pick up many Plains Indian customs. From them they borrowed the horse, buckskin clothing, the skin-covered tipi, rawhide bags and the sun dance. Like their teachers, the Utes and Wind River Shoshonis also became better organized and more warlike.

The name of one Shoshoni should be known to everyone. That was Sacajawea, the Indian woman who helped guide Lewis and Clark across the Rocky Mountains to the Columbia River.

Up in the Plateau country lived well over half of the Basin-Plateau people, divided into some twenty to twenty-five different tribes. This relatively large population was made possible by three great rivers cutting the upland region—the Fraser in Canada and the Columbia and Snake in Washington, Idaho and Oregon. For rivers in this northwest Pacific Coast country meant salmon, salmon by the thousands and hundreds of thousands.

Most tribes tried to secure a foothold on the banks of one of the major rivers where they could fish for salmon. The fishing season ran from May through November. Salmon and other fish were caught by almost every means possible—weirs, funnel-like traps, seines, dip nets, spears, and hooks and lines. They were even sometimes shot with bow and arrow.

Special stands along the banks of the river where fish could be easily netted or speared were highly prized and handed down from father to son.

Salmon and shellfish naturally formed the staple food during the fishing season. But great quantities of salmon were also hung up on wooden racks and dried for use during the winter. Lewis and Clark were amazed at the numbers of these long scaffolds of drying fish in every village they passed.

Many sections of the Plateau were equally rich in wild vegetable foods. From marshy lowlands the Indians dug up camas, kouse and other bulbous roots. These were roasted and either eaten at once or pounded into mush, cooked again, and stored for future use. From the hills and valleys they collected grass seeds, several kinds of berries and pine nuts.

The deer was the most important game animal, but antelope, elk, bear and rabbit were also killed with bow and arrow. Some of the eastern tribes crossed the Rocky Mountains to hunt buffalo.

Most Plateau tribes moved seasonally to take advantage of the different kinds of food. Some built both summer and winter houses. In parts of the area the Indians constructed deep pit houses covered over with earth to keep out the cold. These were entered by ladder through the smoke hole in the roof.

But the most common type of dwelling, particularly in summer, was a large community house built over a shallow excavation. Fifteen feet wide and up to sixty or more feet long, this was constructed of arching poles covered over with mats of tule or cattail. A foot-wide opening down the center of the roof let out the smoke and let in light.

Like their neighbors to the south, these Indians wore as little clothing as possible in the summer. Men wore only a breechcloth of skin, women a similar cloth or apron, adding moccasins, fur leggings, and rabbit-fur robes in cold weather. Some men wore skin caps and some women basketry hats. The eastern tribes, like the Nez Percé, adopted the dress of the Plains Indians, wearing leggings, moccasins, buffalo or elk-skin robes and feathers.

Both men and women generally painted their faces. Some bored holes in their ears for ear ornaments. The French gave the Nez Percé Indians their name, "pierced noses," because of their supposed custom of piercing their noses for ornaments and rings. In Plains Indian sign language everyone knew what tribe was meant when an individual passed his extended index finger under his nose.

The Flathead Indians of Montana got their name not because they flattened their heads, but because they didn't. Their naturally shaped heads just looked deformed in comparison with the artificially tapered skulls of a few of their western Plateau neighbors.

Flathead Indian chief, Montana

These Plateau Indians made no pottery but they did make excellent basketry. Much of their cooking they did by boiling the food in watertight baskets with hot stones.

Wherever possible, villages were built near rivers. These not only furnished the Indians with one of their principal sources of food but also gave them driftwood for both house building and firewood, water and a means of transportation. Most tribes hollowed dugout canoes out of trees or built rafts of logs.

During the eighteenth century, horses began to filter into the Plateau country, probably coming up the western slopes of the Rocky Mountains through the Utes and Shoshonis. The Nez Percé and Cayuse and many other Plateau tribes took enthusiastically to horses. They became excellent horse raisers, specializing in the famous Appaloosa, or polka-dotted horse. The Indians prized these bright-colored horses and developed a lively trade in them. If they couldn't trade for them, the Indians were just as likely to steal them.

Along with the horse, Plateau tribes also acquired many Plains Indian customs. They used the Plains skin tipi when traveling. They adopted the buckskin clothing of the Plains, including the use of beads as decoration on almost everything made of leather. Feather warbonnets came into style, as did also the Plains ideas about warfare.

Although pacifism had been the general rule in the Plateau, a few tribes were warlike. But, with the introduction of horses and guns, they became even more warlike. Raids became common, along with the counting of coups, the taking of scalps and sometimes the capture of slaves.

Prior to this time most Plateau tribes had been loosely organized, with each village more or less independent of the others in the tribe. Chieftainship in a group was generally hereditary, but a chief's authority was largely informal. Now this changed. Tribal organization tightened up. A man's position was determined more by what he did in war than by what family he belonged to.

Religion and ceremonialism were simple in the Plateau area. Perhaps the most important ceremony for most tribes was that held at the time of the catching of the first salmon of the year. Similar ceremonies were sometimes held for the first wild fruits of the season or the first meat. The Indians believed in a number of supernatural beings.

Shamans received their power from guardian spirits. Both men and women could and did become shamans. They cured disease by sucking out the intruding spirit or object, by smoking and by dancing.

In spite of their efforts, people still died. Some tribes held fairly elaborate mourning ceremonies, often with the destruction of the property of the deceased. The corpse was washed, its face painted, and the body dressed in new clothing. It was then usually partially flexed, with the knees drawn up partway towards the chin, and wrapped in mats. Outside the village, the body was laid in a grave, with the head generally pointing downstream. With the body the mourners placed horn cups or spoons or other items as grave offerings.

Lewis and Clark reported a different type of burial along the Columbia River. This was a burial shed in which bodies, wrapped in leather robes, were arranged in rows on boards. A few tribes seem to have practiced cremation of the dead.

The Basin-Plateau area was late in being invaded by white men. But the opening of the California and Oregon trails brought in settlers by the thousands. Some Indians remained peaceful. Others tried to fight back. The most celebrated attempt at revolt was that of Chief Joseph and the Nez Percé in 1877. But that ended in his defeat in Montana, with the captives being sent to Oklahoma. There they stayed for a few years before they were finally allowed to join their relatives on reservations in the Plateau.

8

Seed Gatherers of California

FIVE HUNDRED years ago California was an Indian
paradise. Indians migrated there from all over the country and settled to make the area one of the most densely
populated regions in all of North America north of Mexico.
Anthropologists estimate that there were some 85,000 Indians living in California then.

There were more different languages spoken in this one
small area than in any other. Nearly every major language
family in the United States and Canada was represented
except for the Eskimo.

To account for this wide diversity in peoples and languages something like the following may well have happened. For Asiatic immigrants crossing Bering Strait to
Alaska, the Pacific Coast may have formed a handy route
southward into the United States. Most of them kept right
on going into other parts of the United States or even
into Mexico and South America. But some liked the looks
of the country and stayed.

Archaeologists tell us that Indians have been around

California for thousands of years. Huge shell mounds along the coast confirm this. So do certain inland sites where fluted spearheads suggest that some Indians hunted big-game animals. Even out on Santa Rosa Island, forty-five miles off the southern California coast, it looks as if Indians had been killing and barbecuing pygmy mammoths back in the Ice Age.

By the time the sixteenth century opened, there were some two or three hundred different tribes or triblets living in California. Typical of these were the Chumash, Hupa, Karok, Maidu, Miwok, Modoc, Pomo, Wintun, Yokuts, Yuki, and Yurok. Most of these names probably sound strange to you. They should. Even today not many of these are well known. Only a few California tribes were large. Most of them were small, rarely numbering more than several hundred individuals.

In comparison to the Indians living in the adjacent Southwest or Basin and Plateau regions, California Indians had it easy. For primitive man living conditions were nearly ideal. They didn't have to roast in summer or freeze in winter. They didn't have to work their fingers to the bone to make a living.

Nature furnished them with a mild climate and an abundance of food on the land and in the rivers and ocean.

These Indians knew nothing about farming, but they never needed it. There was more than enough food growing wild all around them. All they had to do was gather it.

Throughout most of California the lowly acorn was the staff of life. Produced in vast quantities by oak trees, acorns were harvested in the fall and carried in baskets to the village and dried. When they were ready to be used, they were cracked open and the nut meats ground to flour.

There was only one thing wrong with acorns. They contained tannic acid, which made them bitter and, in large amounts, even poisonous. The ingenious Indians solved the problem by leaching out the tannic acid. They did this by putting the acorn meal in a scooped-out hollow in clean sand and pouring water on it until the tannic acid was removed by the water.

The meal was then placed in a tightly woven basket and mixed with water to make a thick soup. To cook it the Indians added a few hot stones to the mixture. Sometimes acorn meal was pressed into cakes and baked.

These California Indians didn't live on acorns alone. Acorns gave them starches and fats but they also needed proteins. They got them from a variety of foods. The mountains abounded in deer and elk and bears and rabbits. Lakes and marshes teemed with all kinds of water birds. The rivers were full of fish. Along the sea coast there was an abundance of crabs and crayfish and mussels and abalones. And, if the Indians needed more variety in the vegetable line, the hills and valleys were rich in everything from grass seeds to manzanita berries.

Along the northern California coast salmon took the place of acorns as the staple food. However, acorns were still an important part of the diet.

Although some kind of food was usually available nearly every month of the year, the California Indians believed in storing food away for a rainy day. Nearly every household had its granary for the storage of acorns.

Home life of the Indians of California

California's climate was mild enough that most Indians didn't need substantial houses. The most common type was a domed house, made of a framework of poles covered with a thatch of tules or grass. In the mountains some tribes put up conical huts covered with bark. In the redwood forests along the coast the Hupa and Yurok and other tribes built gabled-roofed houses of redwood planks set vertically in the ground around a twenty-foot-square pit. A round hole two feet in diameter was left in one side for a doorway.

The Maidu Indians of the Sacramento Valley built large, circular, partially underground houses. These were from twenty to forty feet in diameter and from two to three feet deep. The Indians covered a pole and log framework

Pomo Indian hut of tule reeds

with a heavy layer of earth, making a warm house. Several families lived in the larger houses. In the bigger villages there was generally a much larger house set aside as the village dance hall and sweat house.

Down in the Santa Barbara region the average Chumash family didn't like to live alone. A number of related families would get together and erect a building large enough to house all of them. They placed willow poles around a circle of fifty-foot diameter, bent over the tops and tied them together, and covered the whole structure with tule mats. The inside was partitioned off into rooms, one for each family.

Many tule hut villages in the central part of the state also had one or more large, semisubterranean houses roofed with logs and earth. These served as clubhouses or as dance halls. Sweat houses were also features of most villages.

In keeping with the climate, the dress of most California Indians was extremely scanty. As a rule men wore nothing. If the weather turned cool, they wrapped a piece of buckskin around their waists. Women wore two-piece aprons, a small one in front and a large one in back, both suspended from a cord around the waist. Where buckskin was plentiful, aprons were made of this material. Otherwise, they were made of shredded bark, grass or fiber cord. Moccasins were usually worn only for travel. In the colder parts of California both men and women wore deerskin robes or blankets of rabbit fur. Some robes were also made of feathers.

In the technical side of life, the making of implements and utensils, the California Indians would have to be rated well down the scale. Yet they were good in one art, that of making baskets. In this they were so good that they excelled the tribes of any other region in North America, if not in the whole world. They made baskets in every size from that of a pinhead to huge ones ten or more feet in diameter. The stitches on some of these baskets are so fine that you need a magnifying class to see them.

In addition to closely woven, watertight baskets for cooking, they made large storage baskets, bowls, shallow trays, traps, cradles, hats and seed beaters.

To make these baskets they used dozens of different kinds of wild plant stems, barks, roots and leaves. Some of the more common were fern roots, red bark of the redbud, white willow twigs and tule roots, hazel twigs, yucca leaves, brown marsh grass roots and sedge roots.

By combining these different kinds of plants, the Indians were able to make geometric designs on their baskets in red, black, white, brown or tan. Some tribes, particularly the Pomo, decorated their baskets with colorful bird feathers or with shell beads.

In southern California the Chumash and Gabrielino and perhaps other tribes carved jars, figurines and clubs from soapstone. Jars were sometimes decorated with shell beads inlaid in asphalt. In the redwood country the Indians did some carving in wood and elkhorn.

To grind acorns and other nuts and seeds, the Cali-

Courtesy, American Museum of Natural History

Pomo Indian conical twined woven basket

fornia Indians used mortars and pestles and also metates and manos. The latter grinding tools were probably relatively late importations from the Southwest.

In one other art some of these Indians showed a great deal of ingenuity. This was in the making and using of money. The Yurok Indians used dentalium shells as a medium of exchange, recognizing five different grades of shells. In central California clamshell discs strung on cords were used as units of exchange. Red-headed woodpecker scalps also had their value.

From the number of Pacific Coast shells that have turned up in archaeological ruins all over the Southwest, these California Indians must have enjoyed a thriving trade.

For hunting deer and other animals the Indians used the sinew-backed bow. They drove rabbits into nets and trapped and snared birds. They fished with harpoons, nets and shell fishhooks.

For water transportation the northern tribes used small dugout canoes of redwood. In the central area the Indians made crude log or tule rafts to get around the marshes and rivers. Many California Indians were not great travelers. Some rarely ventured more than a few miles from their home village. The Chumash were the exception. Although they lacked big trees, they still built seagoing canoes. They managed this by splitting driftwood into planks, boring holes along the edges, and sewing the planks together with fiber or sinew cords. They made the seams watertight by coating them with asphalt. With these canoes they could travel between the mainland and the offshore islands.

As you might expect, most California Indian tribes lacked complicated social and political organization. Although some tribes had social groupings tracing their descent through the father, many had none. Most lived in small villages of not more than a couple of hundred people. Each village was independent of the others in the tribe. In some villages the office of chief was hereditary; in others it was based on wealth and prestige.

You wouldn't call these Indians warlike. They didn't go around with a chip on their shoulders looking for a fight. Yet each little group was jealous of its slice of territory with its groves of acorn-bearing oaks and its rivers or marshes or seacoast. Some even posted guards against trespassers. If trouble arose between two groups, they would line up and each would select a champion to fight for the honor of their side. Afterwards, there might be considerable speechmaking and arguing before the losers agreed to pay so many shells or other booty to the winners.

California may have been weak in chiefs and politics, but it more than made up for this lack in its medicine men. Among the Maidu, for example, the shaman was more powerful than the chief. Frequently it was the shaman, by revealing the will of the spirits, who chose the next chief.

Shamans gained their power through dreams and visions produced by fasting or taking drugs made of certain wild plants. Many California shamans were specialists. Some controlled the weather. Some cured or prevented snakebite. Some cured other diseases. Some were bear shamans who could turn themselves into bears. If a shaman failed to cure his patient, he received no pay.

The Indians were afraid of shamans who practiced black magic and who could, they believed, kill them if the shamans got hold of pieces of their hair or fingernail clippings or other parts of the body.

Many California Indians could gather enough food during the summer and fall months to last them during the winter and spring. This was the time for ceremonies and dancing, helping to keep the people occupied.

Religion and ceremonialism were extremely simple in many parts of California. Probably the most elaborate ceremonies were those held in the central region. Here religion consisted of a long series of dances and rituals representing mythical or supernatural beings. One of the most widespread ceremonies was that for a girl's coming of age. Boys were also initiated into the male secret society with ceremonial dances. Costuming for some of these dances often included the lavish use of bright-colored feathers and flowers. In northern California the most important ceremonies were associated with salmon fishing, particularly with the catching of the first salmon of the year.

When it came to disposing of their dead, California Indians were about equally divided between cremation and burial. Burial predominated in the north, cremation in the south. The Maidu burned not only the dead but also his house and possessions. Some tribes held elaborate mourning ceremonies for the dead.

The Indians of California were neither rich or poor. Their way of life may have been simple. Yet most of them had one thing that the Indian residents of several other areas didn't have. That was economic security. In fact, these Indians seem to have gotten along very well as long as they were left in peace.

But that situation began to change in 1542. In that year Juan Rodríguez Cabrillo sailed along the Santa Barbara coast and discovered the Chumash Indians. In 1579 Sir Francis Drake landed on the coast north of San Francisco and was greeted by the Indians, probably the Miwok, with elaborate ceremonies. During the next couple of centuries other explorers visited the Indians living along the coast. But their visits were so infrequent and so short that they didn't affect the lives of the Indians.

Courtesy, American Museum of Natural History
Carved mountain goat-horn spoon handles of the Northwest Coast Indians

In 1769, however, the Spanish moved in to stay, founding their first mission at San Diego. Gradually they moved up the coast, establishing twenty other missions, the last just north of San Francisco in 1823.

The Indians were not warlike and the missionaries soon gathered them into villages built around the mission. Here they put clothing on the Indians, taught them Christianity, made them learn farming and other trades, and tried to make them live like civilized people.

But these Mission Indians, as they have since been called, didn't take to their new life. Unaccustomed to heavy clothing, to rigid discipline and to hard work in the fields and shops, their health and spirits failed. Many tried to escape but were caught and brought back. When Mexico gained her independence from Spain, the Mexican government began taking over the missions. Most of the Indians were thrown out to support themselves as best they could. But by that time Mexicans and Americans were moving into California and settling on what had been Indian land. There was no place for most of the Mission Indians.

The gold rush in 1849 didn't make things any better for the central and northern tribes who hadn't been under the influence of the missions. The miners took more land away from the Indians and often hunted them down like wild game.

As the American population increased, the Indians decreased. Today, many tribes are extinct, while others have only a handful of survivors.

9

Woodcarvers and Fishermen of the Northwest Coast

CALIFORNIA MAY have been an Indian Paradise in early days. But the wealthiest Indians, north of Mexico, were those living along what is called the Northwest Coast.

The homeland of these plutocrats was the thousand miles of coast extending from southern Alaska to Puget Sound. Yet their influence reached all the way from the Aleutian Islands in the north to northern California in the south.

These Indians were not only rich, they were extremely unusual. They did everything on a big scale. They built huge gable-roofed wooden houses. They erected giant totem poles in front of their villages. They made equally large dugout canoes. In these they ventured far out to sea to bring back whales and other large sea mammals. They were excellent woodcarvers and painters, decorating nearly everything they made. They were expert weavers and basket-makers. They were warriors, protecting their bodies with armor. They were slave traders. They put on elaborately masked and costumed dramatic and ceremonial performances. They threw huge parties, called potlatches, where everything but the kitchen sink might be given away. They were aristocratic in their outlook, ranking everyone into a series of classes—chiefs, nobles, commoners, slaves—and each class was further graded.

What is remarkable is that the Northwest Coast Indians accomplished all this without the aid of farming or pottery-making, the two things that other tribes seemed to need to become rich city-dwellers.

What made these Indians so wealthy was the Pacific Ocean and the trees. The sea and the rivers furnished them with more food than they could use. The forests furnished an inexhaustible supply of raw materials for their arts and crafts.

In spite of its northern location, this was not a cold country. The warm Japan Current flowed along the curving coastline from Alaska southward, giving the area a moderate climate. But at the same time it also brought lots of rain and fog to the coast and heavy snows to the high mountains.

These were coastal Indians. Hemmed in between the Pacific Ocean and rugged, forest-covered mountains rising abruptly from the water, they lived on the narrow strip of seashore or on the beaches of the hundreds of large and small islands skirting the coast.

More people lived here than in any other area of equal size. According to the best guesses of anthropologists, there

Yurok carved elkhorn spoon and bone money case, northern
California

were over 100,000 Indians crowding this narrow coastal
belt at the time of their discovery.

We don't know too much about the early inhabitants of
the Northwest Coast. Until recently archaeologists hadn't
dug into many of the shell mounds and old village sites
dotting the coast. These show that Indians had been here
for several thousand years. Like their descendants, they
built wooden houses and made their living from the sea.

In the eighteenth century there were half a dozen distinct tribal groups occupying the Northwest Coast from
southern Alaska to Vancouver Island. From north to south
these were the Tlingit, Haida, Tsimshian, Bellacoola,
Kwakiutl, and Nootka.

Although these six tribes may have spoken different
languages, they were quite closely related in their culture,
their way of life. These are the typical Northwest Coast
peoples we shall be talking about in this chapter.

South of them, along the coasts of Washington and Oregon, were a dozen or more other tribes that were influ-

enced by the northern tribes. We might call these imitators or borrowers of Northwest Coast culture. These tribes ranged from the Quileute, Chinook, Tillamook, Coos, and Tolowa to the Yurok in northern California. Living along the Columbia River, the Chinook acted as middlemen in trade between the coastal tribes and the tribes of the interior Plateau area.

Probably most people have heard the word "siwash" attached to this region. This is a mispronunciation of the French "sauvage," meaning savage, a term applied by the French to all Indians. Early in the nineteenth century traders in the Northwest developed a simplified language, called the Chinook jargon, to aid their trading. This was made up of words taken from a number of Indian and European languages. In this jargon, "siwash" was the word for "Indian" as opposed to "white man." Siwash, thus, meant any Indian. There is no Siwash tribe.

The Northwest Coast Indians differed from most other American Indians in the amount of hair on their faces. Many men sported heavy mustaches and some had beards as well. Along with broad heads and broad faces, they also had relatively lighter skins than other Indians. The Indians along the northern part of the coast were taller than their southern relatives.

No Northwest Coast Indian ever had to skip a meal because of a food shortage. Food was probably more abundant here than in any other area in the world.

Like the buffalo among the Plains Indians or corn among the Pueblos, salmon was the staple article of diet. During certain times of the year there were nearly as many salmon in the ocean and rivers as there were grains of sand on the beaches. Halibut, cod, herring and other kinds of fish were almost as numerous.

The Indian fishermen used a wide variety of ingenious methods to catch fish—huge, basketlike traps, pole fences or weirs to turn fish into traps, nets, seines, spears, harpoons, rakes and many specialized types of wooden, bone or horn hooks.

Also from the ocean came sea otters, sea lions, seals and porpoises, used both for food and skins or furs. The Nootka and some of their southern neighbors went far out to sea to harpoon whales. Some other tribes were satisfied to cut up and eat dead whales washed up on the beach.

The Northwest Coast Indians were particularly fond of fish oil. They would often boil herring or cod or other fish and skim off the oil and grease from the surface. But they got most of their oil from the candlefish. This small fish is so oily that, when dried and provided with a wick, it will burn like a candle. Candlefish oil was highly prized by all Northwest Coast tribes. It was also traded far into the interior, the routes over which it was carried being known as "grease trails."

The ocean beaches also furnished the Indians with clams, crabs, mussels and edible eelgrass and seaweed. Supplementing this primarily fishy diet were wild roots, bulbs and berries, and such animals as deer, elk and mountain goats.

During the summer months the Indians were able to accumulate enough fish and other food to last throughout the rest of the year. To store this vast surplus they developed elaborate methods of drying and smoking fish, sea-weed, shellfish, meat and fish oil.

This gave them two things most other Indians never had—a feeling of security and a great deal of leisure time. This they devoted to their arts and crafts, to ceremonies, to feasts and to wars.

Most Northwest Coast tribes could live the year round in permanent villages, built on the shoreline of the main-land near the mouth of a river, on the banks of the larger rivers or on the beaches of offshore islands. A village con-sisted of a number of large wooden houses standing in one or more rows. Their front yard was the ocean, their back yard the forest.

From the back yard came the material to build houses. Most dwellings were huge, varying from thirty to fifty feet in width and from forty to one hundred feet or more in length. Although all Northwest Coast houses were built over a framework of heavy log posts and beams, with cedar planking for the sides and roof, they differed some-what from tribe to tribe.

In the north most houses were solidly put together, with vertical plank side walls and high gable roofs. Many houses had deep pits dug inside the walls, sometimes form-ing a series of three or four benches or steps. For a door-way the Indians cut a round or oval hole through the center post in the gable and facing the beach. Along the southern coast, house builders laid the side planking on horizontally, tying it in place with cedar withes. Such plank-ing could be quickly taken down and put up on another house frame standing at a summer fishing village.

Even in the wet climate of the Northwest Coast such heavy plank houses lasted for half a century or more.

The larger houses accommodated several related families. The house owner and his family generally occupied the left rear corner, with the rest of the families in the other corners or around the side walls. Each family had its own cooking fireplace and low plank beds covered with furs and mats. The center roof boards could be moved with a long pole to let out the smoke. Scattered here and there about the room or stacked up to form partitions were paddles, weapons, fishing gear, firewood and boxes of preserved fish, fish oil and other stored foods.

Just as salmon was the chief food of the Northwest Indians, so the towering cedar tree was the source of much of their raw material. They preferred the cedar to most other trees because its fine-grained wood split straight. Cedar was used to build houses and canoes and boxes and implements and utensils. Its inner bark furnished a fine fiber for clothing and bedding. Its coarser outer bark was woven into mats. Its roots supplied cord and rope and material for basketry. Its dead branches even made good firewood.

Aside from fishing, the major industry of the Northwest Coast Indians was woodworking. Their carpenter's tools may have been limited, but they were master craftsmen in the art of working wood.

It took a lot of hard work to fell a giant cedar. Whenever possible, the Indians made use of trees blown down by storms or washed out by floods. Using sets of wooden wedges and stone hand-hammers, they split logs into planks, smoothing them with adzes and chisels of shell, stone, bone or horn.

By cutting boards partway through and steaming them, they were able to bend them into square or rectangular boxes, joining the wood with wooden pegs or by sewing with spruce roots. Such boxes were watertight enough to cook food by means of red-hot stones dropped in with wooden tongs. Other boxes of various sizes were fitted with lids and used as storage boxes for trinkets, fishing tackle, clothing and food, and as water buckets, drums and coffins.

Courtesy, American Museum of Natural History
Carved ivory shaman's charms of the Tlingit Indians of southern Alaska

From blocks of alder they hollowed out bowls and plates and ladles. Feast dishes might be up to six feet in length and carved into human or animal forms. Horn was also steamed and bent to make dishes and spoons.

With dense forests making travel by foot difficult, the Northwest Coast Indians turned naturally to the water for transportation. They hollowed out cedar logs into dugout canoes, widening them at the top by filling them with water and dropping in hot stones. Projecting bows and sterns were carved separately and sewn in place. These canoes were among the finest made by any primitive people. They were manufactured in all sizes, from small craft for two or three men to huge dugouts fifty to sixty feet long that could carry several tons of goods or fifty or more men.

With the exception of the Nootka, most of the Northwest Coast Indians were not deep-sea navigators. They might make long journeys of several hundred miles up or down the coast; yet they generally kept within sight of shore.

Trees furnished the Indians with bark and roots to make basketry, mats and clothing. Their finest watertight baskets were woven of spruce roots, or of cedar-bark cord and spruce roots, and were often decorated with black, yellow and red designs. Strips of cedar bark were woven into carrying baskets and bags and also into long mats. Cedar bark was shredded, twisted and braided into cord, rope and fishing tackle.

The region's mild climate made warm clothing unnecessary. Actually, clothing was worn more as protection against rain than against cold. In summer most men wore nothing and women only an apron or skirt of shredded cedar bark. Summer and winter, both men and women went bare-legged and barefooted. Doing very little traveling by foot, they didn't have the need for moccasins that their inland relatives did. On ceremonial occasions or in winter a rectangular robe of sea otter fur or woven cedar bark was thrown over the shoulders.

To keep off the rain, both men and women put on tightly woven, flaring capes or ponchos of cedar-bark matting. They protected their heads with conical, wide-brimmed basketry hats.

The best and most colorful blankets were made by the Chilkat division of the Tlingit Indians. These were woven

Courtesy, American Museum of Natural History

Chilkat blanket made by Coast Indians of southern Alaska

of cedar bark and mountain-goat hair, with elaborate designs in white, yellow, black and greenish-blue, with heavy fringes at the sides and bottom. Chilkat robes were traded to the other Northwest Coast Indians, who looked on them as objects of wealth to be worn on ceremonial occasions.

You could almost say a Northwest Coast Indian's life began and ended with cedar bark. As a baby, he was diapered and wrapped in shredded cedar bark. His cradle was padded with the same material. As an adult, most of his clothing was of cedar bark. He ate his meals off a bark tablecloth, sat on a bark mat, and slept on still another. He stored his fishing tackle in a woven bark basket and his carpenter's tools in another. When he died, the chances were good that his body would be wrapped in a mat of cedar bark.

Both men and women were fond of ornaments, wearing necklaces, bracelets, anklets and headbands. They pierced their noses and ears so they could wear pendants of shell, wood, bone or feathers. The women of the northern tribes slit their lower lips for grooved wooden or bone plugs. Some tribes also tattooed designs on their bodies and some painted their faces. A number of the southern tribes thought a deformed head was a mark of distinction. They bound the heads of their youngsters to make them taper upward and backward.

The Northwest Coast Indians not only decorated themselves but also nearly everything else they owned. In addition to the designs on basketry and matting and blankets, they carved or painted designs on their houses, their canoes and canoe paddles, their wooden storage boxes, their burial boxes and grave posts, and their ceremonial masks and head-dresses. Even such strictly utilitarian implements and uten-sils as bone awls and chisels, paintbrushes, fishhooks, spoons, ladles and dishes were frequently decorated with carved or painted designs.

Most of the carvings and paintings were of animals or birds. But you would not be able to recognize them as birds or animals you had seen before. They were not the familiar birds and animals of everyday life. Most were representations of mythical supernatural beings carved in animal or human form.

To add further complications, they were frequently gro-tesquely distorted to fit rectangular boxes or round posts or other odd shapes. And frequently the artist took liber-ties with the anatomy of the animal he was carving, split-ting it in half and showing it as though it were laid out flat. Or he might draw its internal organs. Or he would empha-size two or three features and skip lightly over the rest of the animal. A bear, for example, would be indicated by its short snout, large teeth and claws, and protruding tongue; a beaver by its prominent incisor teeth and its wide, flat tail; a raven by its wings and its long straight beak; an eagle by its down-curving beak; a killer whale by its long dorsal fin.

These weird bird and animal designs were closely tied in with Northwest Coast social and religious organization. Like the cattle brands of the Old West, they represented the owner's family crest or clan membership or mythological genealogy. They were the marks of the owner's rank and wealth and social status.

But the most famous Northwest Coast carvings were huge totem poles. Like the other carvings, these were neither idols nor gods. Some displayed the family crest or told family legends. One of these beautifully carved and painted poles standing in front of a house showed that the owner was a man of wealth and prestige in the community. Other poles were memorial poles to the dead, or burial or grave posts.

Courtesy, American Museum of Natural History

Totem poles on Queen Charlotte Islands, British Columbia

We don't know how long these Indians have been erecting totem poles. Like anything else made of wood, totem poles don't last too many years in this wet climate. Most poles decayed and fell down in fifty to seventy-five years. Once they were on the ground, the Indians frequently cut them up for firewood, leaving nothing behind for archaeologists to find. In the latter part of the eighteenth century the first European explorers reported seeing elaborately carved and painted house posts and grave poles. With the acquisition of iron axes and chisels, the Indians began building bigger and better poles. Totem poles reached their peak during the nineteenth century, declining rapidly after 1890. Today the art is almost lost.

Carving and putting up a totem pole fifty to sixty feet long and five feet in diameter was an expensive as well as a long and difficult task. Only the wealthy could afford one. Professional artists had to be hired to do the actual carving and painting. Like house posts and wooden boxes, the earlier totem poles were painted in native colors, generally red, black and white. When commercial paints were finally introduced, the artists seized upon them and splashed a rainbow of colors over totem poles, houses, canoes and boxes.

Like everything else about the Northwest Coast way of life, social, political and religious organization was extremely complicated. There was no single pattern that all tribes followed. The northern tribes traced their descent through the female line, but most of the southern tribes traced descent bilaterally.

Some northern tribes, as the Tlingit and Haida, were

divided into two groups, into one of which every individual was born. The Haidas called these groups Ravens and Eagles. A man had to take his wife from the opposite division. When a man was a Raven, his wife was an Eagle. Since descent was matrilineal, their children were also Eagles.

Each of these divisions was further subdivided into a number of smaller groups or clans. These formed the tribe's major social units, each with its own name, its own crest and ceremonies, its own chiefs and subchiefs.

Other northern tribes had a fourfold or sixfold division into clans named after birds and animals. Most southern tribes lacked clans, organizing themselves into large, related families, each with its own land and ceremonies and chiefs.

Northwest Coast Indians may have differed in their social setup, yet all were aristocratic, proud of their ancestry. They didn't believe in democracy. Only wealth and property and family connections counted.

Technically, slaves did not form a class. They were war captives and had no rights at all. Like any other piece of property, they could be bought and sold and even killed.

In most tribes social status depended upon a combination of heredity and wealth. The social prestige of a woman, as well as that of her husband and children, was high or low depending upon the amount of wealth that was exchanged between the two families at the time of marriage. If a man could afford the added expense, he might have more than one wife. A family's wealth was counted

Courtesy, American
Museum of Natural
History
Engraved copper of the
Haida Indians, Queen
Charlotte Islands, British
Columbia

in its stores of food, furs, mats, Chilkat blankets, carved boxes, slaves and "coppers."

Coppers were large, shield-shaped plates hammered out of chunks of native copper received in trade from the Copper River Athabascan Indians. Each of these painted and engraved plaques had a name and a history, its value depending on this history and the amount for which it had last been sold. Some coppers were worth thousands of dollars. As late as 1893, one was valued at 7,500 woolen trade blankets.

At the top of the social ladder were the chiefs. The owner of a house was a house chief. Generally the richest and most powerful house chief would also be the village chief. Close relatives of the chief ranked just below him, followed by poor relatives of the nobles. Below them were middle-class people who, while not of high birth, did own some property. Through marriage with a higher-ranking person or through the accumulation of property, an individual could raise himself up the scale.

No matter how high a standing a chief might have, he was always on the lookout for ways to push the family prestige another rung up the ladder. He might do this by giving a formal banquet or having a potlatch, a word from the Chinook jargon meaning "giving." When a chief gave a potlatch, all his relatives chipped in to help gather a store of food, baskets, shells, boxes and other articles of value. Following a lavish feast, at which guests were seated according to their rank, the host distributed gifts to the guests. Even though he might give away nearly everything he owned, his prestige was secure. Sooner or later the receivers of the gifts were obligated to return them with heavy interest.

Most potlatches were given for some definite purpose, as to mourn the death of a chief or other important person, to honor a new chief or to celebrate betrothals and marriages. A chief might also give a face-saving potlatch to offset some misadventure.

A chief was never backward about boasting of his exploits and ridiculing his rivals. Sometimes, to show his disdain for wealth, a Kwakiutl chief would chop a canoe into pieces or burn stores of fish oil or break a copper or kill a slave.

Wealth, you might say, was accumulated only to be given away or destroyed. One quick way to acquire more property was through raids. Most Northwest Coast tribes were warlike. Some wars were fought for revenge, but many had only one objective—plunder in land and goods and slaves.

The Indians fought with bows and arrows, spears and slings. Good stone was scarce, and arrows were commonly tipped with bone, shell, or copper points. For hand-to-hand combat, they used clubs of wood or whalebone and daggers with stone, bone or copper blades. Nor did they neglect defense. Unlike most American Indians, they wore various kinds of armor. The simplest was a sleeveless shirt made of several thicknesses of leather. A heavier tunic consisted of flat or round wooden rods sewed together with rawhide. The head was protected with a wooden helmet and the face with wooden pieces shaped like a visor.

Some raids might cover several hundred miles up or down the coast. But the rewards in plunder and slaves could be huge for a successful raid.

As with other American Indians, religion played an important part in the everyday life of these people. They believed in a host of supernatural beings. Most of these were nature spirits, particularly fish, animals and birds. They had numerous myths and tales about the activities of these humanlike spirits.

Winter was the time for their major ceremonies—the giving of names to children of important families, initiation into the secret societies, memorial services for the dead, the building of new houses, the erection of totem poles and burial posts. Although these were primarily religious, most of them were also highly dramatic performances. Settings were elaborate and the actors were masked and costumed to represent supernatural beings. Many of the carved and painted wooden masks had movable eyelids and lips to heighten the dramatic effect. Feasting, singing, dancing and the giving of gifts usually accompanied each performance.

Among many tribes the shaman rivaled the chiefs in power and prestige. The medicine men gained their magic power through the aid of supernatural helpers, whose

Courtesy, Bureau of American Ethnology, Smithsonian Institution

Shaman's mask and killer whale crest hat of the Tlingit Indians

masks they wore during curing ceremonies. Shamans were believed able to cure disease, to foretell the future, to bring salmon into the rivers, to locate stranded whales and to counteract sorcery.

When death came, the body was generally taken out of the house through a hole in the side wall to fool the ghost of the dead. Most of the southern tribes buried their dead in wooden boxes high up in trees or in caves. The northern tribes cremated their dead, putting the burned bones in

Courtesy, American Museum of Natural History
Model of Haida shaman's grave, Queen Charlotte Islands, British Columbia

raised boxes or in burial columns. The bodies of shamans, however, were placed in grave houses on platforms. The personal property of the deceased was either buried with him or burned. All of the tribes erected carved and painted memorial posts for chiefs and other prominent citizens.

Europeans didn't discover the Northwest Coast until nearly the middle of the eighteenth century. First to come were Russian explorers in 1741. A boat they sent ashore in Tlingit territory never returned. In 1774 Spaniards sailed along the southern coast, and in 1778 Captain Cook also visited the coast. Discovering that sea-otter skins were highly prized by the Chinese, traders by the dozen soon were coming annually to do business with the Indians. In 1799 the Russians built a fort near the present-day town of Sitka, Alaska. Two years later the Tlingit attacked and destroyed the fort. In 1804 the Russians came back and built another fort, which they managed to hold. During the next half-century the Hudson's Bay Company established a chain of trading posts all along the coast.

The fur traders brought more wealth to the already rich Northwest Coast Indians. Their woodworking, their totem-pole art, their entire way of life reached a brilliant peak, only to fade quickly under the advancing tide of civilization.

10

Hunters and Fishers of the Northern Forests

FROM THE mild Northwest Coast and its thousands of wealthy Indians, we turn to a region where winters were long and cold and its inhabitants few and poor.

Lying between the frozen tundra of the Arctic and the grasslands of southern Canada, the Mackenzie-Yukon area stretches from Hudson Bay northwestward through Canada to the Yukon Valley in Alaska. Much of it is flat or rolling country, heavily forested with pine, spruce, birch and poplar, but there are mountains in the western part of the area. It is also a watery land, a land of rivers and lakes and marshes.

Its climate is nothing to brag about. Winters are long and severe, the temperature dropping to fifty degrees below zero. Snowfall ranges from light to heavy. Summers are often warm but plagued with biting flies and huge mosquitoes.

As you might expect, this was the most thinly inhabited area in North America. Five hundred years ago it was home for not many more than thirty thousand hardy nomads. Even now very few white men attempt to live there year-round.

The unique thing about this area is that it was settled exclusively by Athabascan-speaking Indians. We have run across these tribes before—the Navaho and Apache in the Southwest, the Tlingit, Haida and Tsimshian along the Northwest Coast, and the Hupa, Kato and other tribes in California. These either didn't like their cold northern homeland or couldn't get along with their neighbors. At any rate they moved out, perhaps a thousand, perhaps two thousand, years ago.

Actually, it is possible that none of the Athabascans had lived too long in Alaska and Canada. Anthropologists tell us that their ancestors were the last Indians to migrate from Asia to the New World. To corroborate this, a few linguists have hinted that Athabascan is distantly related to certain languages of eastern Asia. Just when these Athabascan-speaking Indians crossed Bering Strait we can't say. The best guess is that they arrived in Alaska some time around 1000 B.C., give or take a few hundred years.

Like the Greeks, the Athabascans may have come bearing gifts. Some archaeologists think the newcomers brought with them tailored skin and fur clothing, moccasins, the snowshoe and toboggan, and the sinew-backed bow, perhaps even the first bow and arrow to be used in the New World. It is only fair to state, however, that not all archaeologists agree with this. Some believe the Eskimo were the first to introduce tailored clothing to America.

Several score Indian tribes or bands occupied this area

in the sixteenth century. Chief among these were the Hare, Carrier, Oogrib, Yellowknife, Chipewyan, Beaver, Slave, Kaska, Sekani, Kutchin, Tanana, Tanaina and Ingalik.

Some anthropologists would include in this culture area the Algonkian-speaking Cree, Montagnais and Naskapi living in Labrador and around the southern end of Hudson Bay. The way of life of these tribes, as we mentioned in Chapter Three, was similar in many respects to that of the Indians of the Mackenzie-Yukon area. However, we shall limit our discussion to the Athabascan tribes.

These northern Athabascans were simple hunting and fishing peoples. They had no knowledge of farming. For many Athabascans, life revolved around the caribou, the main source of their food supply. What the buffalo was to the Plains Indians the caribou was to most of these Indians.

Hunting caribou was frequently a community venture. There are different kinds of caribou. Some are more or less solitary animals, spending the entire year in the woods. Others live in the forests in winter but migrate northward in great herds to summer feeding grounds on the Arctic tundra, returning to the woodlands in late autumn.

Caribou were hunted in several different ways. A group of hunters might surround a herd and drive it into an enclosure or trap, where the animals could be speared. Caribou were also chased into rivers or lakes, where they could be followed in canoes and more easily killed. In winter, a hunter on snowshoes could run down a caribou floundering in deep snow. Some tribes used rawhide snares to trap caribou as well as smaller animals. Moose, musk-

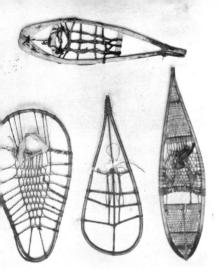

Snowshoes of British Columbia Indians

oxen, bear, deer, elk, beaver, marmots and hares were also hunted. The Hare Indians got their name from their dependence on the hare.

Nearly all tribes supplemented their caribou and other meat with fish. Salmon, in fact, was the staple food for the Carrier and other tribes living along the headwaters of the Yukon and other rivers flowing into the Pacific. The Indians collected what wild plant foods they could find, but, with the exception of berries, these were not too plentiful.

To tide them over the lean months of the year they stored food on high platforms or in underground caches. In summer this surplus was either smoked or dried; in winter Nature provided her own freezer.

Although game was generally fairly abundant, it varied widely with the seasons. Many Indians lived not far above a bare subsistence level. When game was scarce, famine was not uncommon. At such times families were sometimes forced to abandon their aged or sick members who were no longer able to look after themselves.

Following the caribou and other migratory game animals kept the northern Indians on the move much of the year. Most of them could not live in permanent villages and built conical, tipi-like lodges. Some tribes covered their pole tipis with caribou skins. Those who couldn't afford skin covered them with bark or brush. In summer, when the Indians were following the caribou, many of them put up crude, temporary shelters of brush, bark or skins. In winter, tribes on the Mackenzie River frequently built rectangular huts of poles and brush. Along the Yukon River, the Kutchin and their neighbors built houses of logs, weatherproofing them with banked up moss and dirt. Some tribes living in British Columbia constructed plank houses like those of the Northwest Coast, even carving the posts with family crests.

Throughout the Mackenzie-Yukon area, clothing was made of skin. For men the usual costume consisted of a long shirt, breechcloth, leggings and moccasins, all of dressed caribou skin. The soft-soled moccasins were frequently sewed to the bottoms of the hide leggings. Women wore shirtlike dresses, leggings and moccasins. Both wore fur robes, fur caps and fur mittens in cold weather. While the Indians in most other areas went around lightly clad in summer, many northerners covered nearly every inch of skin as protection against flies and mosquitoes.

According to a Canadian anthropologist, it took from eight to eleven caribou skins to outfit a man from head to foot and as many more to make his lodge cover, traps, nets and other utensils. The Hare Indians, not being able to get enough caribou skins, often used rabbit fur for many of their garments.

Many Indians ornamented their clothing with dyed porcupine-quill or moose-hair embroidery or with painted decorations. Both men and women frequently wore bracelets, belts and armbands of leather embroidered with porcupine quills. Some tribes painted their faces and bodies and some, perhaps influenced by the Eskimo, practiced tattooing.

To live, these people had to be able to move camp quickly. In summer they used the portable, bark-covered canoe to get around on the region's many rivers and lakes. Since birch trees were scarce in parts of the far north, some of them had to fall back on spruce bark. In winter snowshoes and toboggans were equally useful for fast travel over the snow and ice. Snowshoes varied in shape from tribe to tribe. Most Athabascans preferred the long, narrow style to the broad, oval form used in the Northeast.

Toboggans were made of long, smooth planks lashed side by side and turned up at the front end. Even though all families had dogs, they used them for hunting rather than for pulling loaded toboggans over the snow. The Kutchin Indians in Alaska borrowed the sled from the neighboring Eskimo, but it was drawn by women, not by dogs.

Like most nomads, the Athabascans had to travel light and couldn't afford the luxury of owning too many possessions. For their implements and utensils most tribes used skin, bark, wood, bone and horn more than they did stone. Many of their dishes, trays, buckets and other containers were made of light bark, their bags of skin or fur. Spruce roots were woven into cooking baskets. Spoons and ladles were carved from wood.

Their only stone implements were spearheads and arrowheads and knives. Some tribes, however, used bone or antler points on their spears and arrows and beaver teeth or moose horn for knives. The Yellowknives, as their name implies, hammered chunks of native copper into knife blades.

The one thing every well-run Athabascan household was never without was a roll of rawhide cord, called "babiche" by the early French traders. Babiche was usually cut spirally from caribou skin laid out flat. It took a steady hand to produce a long, thin strip of even rawhide. Babiche was used for the lacings of snowshoes, fishing tackle, nets, bags, rope and for all kinds of bindings and lashings. Every hunter or traveler carried a roll in his overnight kit.

Also like most nomads, the Athabascans didn't go in for complicated social and political life. There was no tribal organization, no tribal chief. Tribes were split up into a number of bands, each of which roamed over a large territory. Even leadership of a band was highly informal, the best hunter generally having the biggest following. During much of the year small groups of from one to four or five families wandered the forests. Occasionally these groups might get together for feasting or trading. But most of the time they were too busy scratching for a living to think about anything but food.

Now and then they did take time out for a little raiding. These were small-scale affairs for loot or captives or revenge. Sometimes the Athabascans fought the Eskimo; sometimes they fought each other. The Yellowknives, for example, seem to have warred against their neighbors, the Slaves, Dogribs and Hares. But in 1823 the Dogribs rose up and nearly wiped out the Yellowknives. To the south, the Algonkian Crees were continually trying to push up into Athabascan territory.

Within most Athabascan tribes in the Mackenzie-Yukon area descent was generally traced through both parents. More attention, perhaps, was given to the father's side of the family because the wife usually went to live in her husband's band.

Other Athabascan tribes, like the Carrier and Kaska and Kutchin, living in British Columbia and Alaska, where they were influenced by the Northwest Coast Indians, had more elaborate social systems. They divided people into classes and had clans with descent through the female line. They also threw potlatches and laid great emphasis on rank and prestige and wealth.

Generally a prospective bridegroom worked for the girl's parents for a year before the actual marriage feast. After that the man and his in-laws avoided speaking to each other. As in most other areas, a man might have more than one wife if he could afford it. Some Athabascans wrestled each other, with the winner getting the loser's wife.

Athabascan religion was as simple and uncomplicated as its social organization. Most people believed in a multitude of supernatural beings or nature spirits, including giants, monsters and demons. Rituals and ceremonies, except in tribes influenced by the Northwest Coast, were few and far between. Every misfortune was laid at the door of witchcraft, or offended spirits.

The most influential individual in almost every band was the shaman. His singing and dancing and feats of magic entertained as well as awed his audience. He was expected to bring game animals into the region as a food supply. He was called upon to do everything from driving away a threatening storm to curing the sick. Both sickness and death were believed due to sorcery.

These Athabascans didn't bury their dead in the ground. Much of the time it was frozen too hard. Some tribes wrapped their dead in skins and placed the bodies in trees or on scaffolds. Some, like the Slaves, built a small hut over the remains and left them. Other tribes, perhaps influenced by the Northwest Coast, cremated their dead. The Carrier Indians got their name from the custom of forcing widows to carry on their backs the charred bones of their dead husbands.

European traders began invading the northern forests during the seventeenth century. Their coming changed the Athabascan way of life. The Indians trapped mink, beaver and fox, exchanging the furs for firearms, blankets, metal tools and flour and other foods. White man's diseases cut down their numbers. Yet today thousands of Athabascans are still living in the far north, hunting, fishing and trapping in land no one else seems to want.

11

Eskimo Hunters of the Arctic

NORTH OF the Arctic Circle lived the most unique and in many ways the most unusual people in the New World—the Eskimo.

Their home was the six thousand miles of Arctic coast stretching from southwestern Alaska all the way across northern Canada to the eastern shores of Greenland. As large as their territory was, you could have put all the Eskimo into an area the size of the Los Angeles Memorial Coliseum and still have had room left over. Anthropologists estimate that there were about 90,000 Eskimo at the time of their discovery. From one end of the Arctic to the other the various Eskimo tribes were remarkably alike in looks, language and way of life.

Some anthropologists believe the Eskimo were the last immigrants to cross Bering Strait from Asia to North America, following closely on the heels of the Athabascans.

Unlike the Athabascans, however, the Eskimo were not Indians. Physically, the Eskimo stand apart from the other inhabitants of the New World. Most Eskimo are short. They

Eskimo man, Alaska

have extremely broad, flat faces with prominent cheekbones. Their noses are long and narrow and their eyes
are also narrow, frequently showing the distinctive Mongoloid fold. They look more like the Chukchis and other
Mongoloid groups in northeastern Siberia than they look
like their Indian neighbors in Alaska and Canada. Their
speech is also more closely related to certain Siberian languages than it is to any of the American Indian languages.

In fact, until recent years the Eskimo and their Siberian
relatives used to visit each other back and forth across
Bering Strait.

The ancestors of the modern Eskimo probably paddled
over from Asia in skin boats or walked across the ice

before the beginning of the Christian Era. It is highly probable that the Eskimo brought with them such things as tailored skin clothing, the bow drill, the double paddle, the socketed harpoon, and the dog-drawn sled. Archaeologists have found their villages on Big and Little Diomede Islands in the middle of Bering Strait and on the shores of the Alaskan mainland. These early Eskimo lived in small, square or rectangular, partly underground houses. These houses had floors paved with stone and walls and roofs of whalebone and driftwood covered over with sod. Entrance was by a long, low tunnel.

Digging in the Arctic is no easy job. The ground is permanently frozen. Even in summer it thaws only to a depth of one foot to a foot and a half. When exposed to the air overnight, from one to three inches of this frozen ground thaws out. So archaeologists have to dig in thin layers, waiting patiently until the next layer thaws. Yet their efforts are richly rewarded as freezing helps preserve implements and utensils that would otherwise decay and be lost.

The north Alaskan Eskimo peoples of two thousand years ago were great artists. Many of their tools, hunting and fishing equipment, and ornaments were made of walrus ivory or of bone. On the smooth surfaces of these they carved straight and curved lines, dots, circles and other designs. Some of this delicate engraving is unsurpassed in North America.

Some early Eskimo villages were huge. At Point Hope, two hundred miles north of Bering Strait on the Alaskan coast, archaeologists uncovered a buried town of nearly eight hundred houses arranged in five long rows. They also dug up an Eskimo cemetery about a mile from the village. All the graves were shallow, probably because of the difficulty of excavating the frozen ground. Some burials had been covered over with log tombs. Several skeletons buried in the tombs had received unusual treatment. The Eskimo had equipped the skulls with carved ivory eyeballs inlaid with jet pupils and carved ivory mouth covers. One skull had ivory nose plugs carved with bird figures.

As the population increased, the Eskimo gradually spread out from Bering Strait along the Alaskan coast. Some went south, winding up on the southern Alaska coast and out on the grassy Aleutian Islands. Today the Aleuts speak an Eskimoan language, but the relationship is so remote that Aleuts and Eskimos cannot understand each other. Other Eskimos followed the coast northward and eastward, reaching across northern Canada as far as Greenland and Newfoundland.

Some of the Eskimo lived in a land of cold and snow and ice. Their homeland was the nearly treeless Arctic plain bordering the ocean. Winters were long, with almost continuous darkness for three or four months. The sea and the rivers were frozen solid for well over half the year. Summers might be warm but they were extremely short. In many places snow was liable to fall at any time, even in the middle of summer. Along the coast snows were rarely heavy. But they were frequently accompanied by freezing blizzards that piled the snow in drifts and dropped temperatures to well below zero.

The Arctic was not an easy country in which to live. It

offered very little in the way of comforts. Yet it did have its advantages. The Eskimo didn't have to fight anybody for the land. No one else wanted it. And the cold water brought in fish and sea mammals by the thousands. The Eskimo were able to survive because of these sea mammals and because of numerous ingenious tools and implements which they either invented or borrowed from other Asiatic hunters.

The Eskimo called themselves Inuit, which means "the people." The name Eskimo, meaning "eaters of raw flesh," was given to them by the Cree and other Algonkian-speaking tribes in southern and eastern Canada.

The term aptly fitted the Eskimo. The Arctic had few edible wild fruits and plants, and the Eskimo in the High Arctic were forced to live almost exclusively on meat. Fully half of this they ate raw, including fat and internal organs. To us this may not sound appetizing. But only in this way could the Eskimo get their daily supply of vitamins. The Eskimo's capacity for meat was almost unbelievable. A hungry hunter could stow away from six to eight or even ten pounds of meat without stopping.

The Eskimo made their living from the ocean. The sea furnished them with most of their food and also the raw materials for their implements and utensils.

During the short summers many Eskimo, particularly those in Canada, traveled inland to the barren tundra to hunt caribou. Polar bears were also a favorite food. Other Eskimo living in Alaska around the mouth of the Yukon River caught salmon and hunted birds and collected their eggs.

But during most of the year most Eskimo depended on the mammals of the sea, hunting seals and walruses and whales. The flesh and blubber of these furnished the bulk of their food and the fuel for cooking, heating and lighting. Walruses and seals provided skins for clothing, boat coverings, all kinds of lines and ropes and harness, and bone and ivory for weapons and utensils. From the sea also came their only supply of wood, driftwood.

The Eskimo hunted with bows and arrows, spears and spear throwers, and harpoons. Because of the scarcity of wood, bows were frequently made of three pieces of bone or caribou antler riveted together and backed by sinew.

But perhaps their most important weapon was the harpoon. This was not a new weapon. Two thousand years earlier their ancestors had hunted seals with similar harpoons. The harpoon was a compound spear made up of a bone or ivory head mounted on a bone foreshaft lashed to a ball-and-socket joint on a wooden main shaft. Cords bound it together until it struck the target. Then the joint loosened, freeing the shaft and keeping it from breaking. The barbed head, with attached rawhide line, turned crosswise in the prey and held it fast. Floats of inflated sealskin tied to the line helped exhaust the animal. All the hunter had to do was wait until the seal or walrus had tired itself out and then spear it and haul it in. To get more force, harpoons were often hurled by means of the spear thrower or throwing board.

In winter hunters harpooned seals when they came up for air at their breathing holes in the ice. In spring they stalked seals and walruses over the floating ice. In summer they went out to sea in their skin boats to harpoon seals and walruses and even whales.

These Eskimo skin-covered boats were models of ingenuity. There were two kinds, the kayak and the umiak. The kayak was the small one-man canoe made of a light wood and bone frame completely decked over with skin except for the round hatch where the occupant sat. When he had fitted his waterproof jacket around this opening, the kayak was unsinkable. Using his double-bladed wooden paddle, he could even right himself if the kayak turned upside down.

The umiak was called the woman's boat. Larger than the kayak, it was a broad, open boat made of heavy walrus hide stretched over a frame of whalebone or driftwood. Propelled by oars or paddles, the umiak could carry a large number of people or a sizable cargo. When used for transport, it was handled by women. Occasionally a group of men would use the umiak to hunt whales.

In winter, when the ocean and rivers were frozen over and kayaks and umiaks had to be stored away, the Eskimo used the dogsled to get around over the snow and ice. In building sleds, the resourceful Eskimo pieced out their small bits of driftwood with bone and ivory and whale jawbones, lashing them together with rawhide thongs. This made a strong yet flexible sled, able to run over rough ice without breaking. The Eskimo even reduced friction by icing their runners. To guide their sleds many Eskimo added handles of antler at the back.

Sleds were pulled by five or six dogs, often fewer, each hitched to the sled by its own separate trace. They were spread out in a fan formation, with the leader in the center and a few feet ahead of the others. The dog team linked in line that we see in the movies is an Indian and white-man style used in forests or deep snow. These big, slant-eyed Eskimo huskies could pull a loaded sled at the rate of four or five miles an hour for ten or twelve hours a day. The dogs were expensive to own, however, as they had to be fed enormous quantities of seal meat and fish during the long winters. For that reason few families, until recent years, had more than four or five dogs.

But to survive in the Arctic the Eskimo needed more than food and transportation. He had to have shelter, some method of heat and warm clothing.

No one has to be told that the Eskimo lived in snow-houses called igloos. Some Eskimo did. But more of them didn't. Over half of the Eskimo had never even seen a snowhouse. Actually, snowhouses were common only in the Canadian Arctic. Some of the other Eskimo put up small snowhouses when they were on the trail, but these were only temporary structures.

Many Eskimo lived in skin-covered pole tents in the summer when they were out on the tundra chasing caribou and other game. But for their winter dwellings along the seashore they wanted something warmer and more perma-nent. They built these of whatever material was handy—stone, earth or driftwood. Whalebones were highly prized for roof beams. Frequently houses were partly excavated in the sides of gravel banks for greater warmth. Most houses had an outer covering of banked-up earth or sod and an inner lining of skins. Around the inner walls of the house were platforms raised several feet above the floor. These were covered with furs and used for lounging or working or sleeping. The house might even have a window or skylight made of the translucent membrane of a seal's intestine. For an entrance they added on a long tunnel, making it low and sloping it upward to keep out the wind and cold air. Most entrances opened toward the sea.

In the central Canadian Arctic the Eskimo built dome-shaped snowhouses of blocks of hard-packed snow. With a bone snow knife, the homebuilder cut large rectangular blocks of snow. Working from the inside, he laid these out in a circle, tipping each succeeding layer a little inward as it spiraled upward toward the top. A single block, shaped to fit, closed the apex of the dome. The builder then cut a hole in the side and let himself out, constructing with more blocks a long, low tunnel out from this entrance. As in other winter houses, there were raised platforms of snow at the sides and back and windows of pieces of gut or slabs of ice.

The only drawback to the snowhouse was that it wasn't permanent. It melted with the coming of warm weather. But it could be rebuilt once the first snowfall brought a fresh supply of building materials. And it was particularly useful to hunters or travelers caught in a sudden blizzard. They could put together a snowhouse in minutes and wait out the storm in comparative comfort.

Even with such nearly airtight houses, the Eskimo couldn't live in the Arctic without heat. In a literally woodless country, the ingenious Eskimo learned how to burn

oil with a twisted moss wick in a shallow soapstone dish.
Sea mammals furnished the oil, the best coming from the
blubber of seals. Temperatures outside might fall to thirty
or forty degrees below zero, yet two or three of these seal-
oil lamps would comfortably heat a fifteen- to twenty-foot-
square house. The air might be cool at floor level. But up
on the platforms it was warm, warm enough so that the
occupants usually stripped to the waist. If it got too hot
and stuffy, a piece of fur plugging up a small vent in the
ceiling could be removed. This would draw cool, fresh air
up into the house from the tunnel.

The same seal-oil flame also lighted the house during
the long winter days and nights of darkness. Whatever
food wasn't eaten raw was boiled in a soapstone kettle
suspended over another one of these handy seal-oil lamps.
An equally important use of the lamp was to melt snow
and ice for drinking water. Water was scarce and the
Eskimo wasted very little for washing.

The storage of meat and other foods was easy for the
Eskimo. Along the entrance tunnel of each house there
would be an antechamber or two or maybe a built-in locker
which would keep meat as cold as any modern deep freeze.

To protect his own body from the cold the Eskimo
dressed from head to foot in furs. Clothing styles were
similar for both men and women. For an upper garment
they wore jackets, the well-known parka complete with
sleeves and a hood. The woman's parka was made bigger
in back so that a baby could ride safely inside. The
Eskimo, unlike the Indians, did not use the cradleboard.
Both sexes also wore fur trousers, the man's reaching to

the knee, the woman's shorter. They protected their legs and feet with fur stockings and long fur boots. Fur mittens completed the costume. In winter they doubled their clothing, wearing the inner set with the fur against the body and the outer set with the fur side out. For added warmth they often stuffed dry grass into their boots. The inner jacket lacked a hood. That and a short pair of

Dress of the Alaskan Eskimo

trousers formed the standard summer attire. To keep from getting wet they might put on watertight clothing of seal or whale gut.

To prevent snow blindness, the Eskimo wore wood or ivory goggles, with narrow slits to cut down the reflected sunlight. In some areas men out in kayaks frequently used eyeshades or visors.

Eskimo women were expert fitters and tailors. Nothing we have been able to make today can equal their Arctic clothing for comfort and warmth. These seamstresses preferred to work with caribou skin because it was warmer, lighter and more flexible than sealskin. On occasion they made clothing of polar bear fur. For sewing, they used split sinew thread, eyed needles of bone and thimbles of thick hide. They could even sew a watertight seam. Often they decorated clothing by using skins of contrasting colors. Some women's parkas were fringed; others had a fur border.

The Eskimo wore very few ornaments, perhaps because most of the time clothing covered most of their bodies. Women, less often men, might sport a necklace or bracelet of fish vertebrae or bear or seal teeth. Women did, however, tattoo their faces. Women left their hair long, either doing it up close to their heads or braiding it. Men cut their hair in some fashion, generally leaving bangs in the front.

The Eskimo were great gadgeteers. They loved to tinker, to make all sorts of odds and ends of tools and appliances. One of the early traders tells of giving a broken watch to an Eskimo friend. The Eskimo had never seen a watch before and didn't know how it worked. Yet he began to tinker and within a couple weeks had it running again.

Owing to the scarcity of wood, the Eskimo had to use ivory, bone, horn, stone and skin for most of their implements. A whale, for example, was a gold mine of material. Its flesh furnished food for many a feast, its blubber oil for lamps. Whale bones were valuable for household utensils, its ribs for roof beams. The intestines served for waterproof clothing and food containers. Baleen, the horny material from the whale's mouth, was made into harpoon lines and seal nets. Baleen, incidentally, was formerly used by us to make corset stays.

The Eskimo tool bag included the usual knives, scrapers, adzes, hammers, wedges and awls. In addition, they made a bewildering variety of hooks, drills, needles, ivory needle cases, dippers, spoons, combs, back scratchers, carved soapstone dishes, swivels and buckles for dog harness, harpoon points, carved ivory minnows for artificial bait, walrus-tusk ice picks, walrus shoulder-blade snow shovels and countless other implements.

Without the bow drill to bore holes in bone and ivory, the Eskimo couldn't have made many of his tools. This unique appliance had a mouthpiece at one end of the shaft and a stone drill at the other. The operator held the shaft firm by gripping the mouthpiece between his teeth and rotated the drill by a small bow whose cord was wrapped loosely about the shaft. The bow drill also came in handy for starting fires by friction, although many Eskimo frequently made fire from the sparks produced by striking together flint and iron pyrites.

Some Eskimo groups in Canada pounded nuggets of native copper into knives and other tools. And the Eskimo around Bering Strait used a small amount of iron that probably came across from Asia by trade. But most of the Eskimo were strictly Stone Age people.

The ingenious Eskimo even used the freezing weather to help make implements. One of their fiendish trapping devices consisted of a piece of whalebone sharpened at both ends, tightly coiled, and frozen in a chunk of fat or meat. When a wolf came by and gulped it down, the meat thawed and the whalebone uncoiled, stabbing the animal from within.

The Eskimo may not have gone in for ornaments or for decorating their bodies. But, like their ancestors, they were artistically inclined, carving or engraving naturalistic and geometric designs on most of their bone and ivory implements and utensils.

When it came to politics and social life, the Eskimo were individualists. They themselves recognized that they were divided into over a hundred different tribal groups. But there was little or no feeling of tribal unity, no tribal chiefs. The nearest thing to a permanent unit was the family. Several families, generally but not always related, gathered together to form a band. Most groups were small, rarely exceeding more than a hundred individuals and frequently fewer. The Eskimo had no clans or other relationship groups. They reckoned kinship much like we do, following both sides of the family.

There was no real village chief. If there was any one leader or headman in a group, he would be the best hunter.

He didn't inherit his position or get elected to it. He was looked up to because of his skill and experience. People would listen to a good hunter but not to a poor one.

Even though the Eskimo were individualists, Arctic life demanded close cooperation by the members of a village. Food was shared. A family never went hungry as long as others in the village had food. A successful hunter divided his catch with others. Next time he might not be so lucky and would be thankful to be on the receiving end.

Until recent years there were no rich or poor in the average Eskimo settlement. Except for differences in the quality of their implements and utensils, each family had about the same standard of living.

Marriage among the Eskimo was a simple affair, with no formal wedding ceremony. A man might have several wives and a woman could have more than one husband. But monogamy was the general rule. Divorce was equally simple and fairly common, particularly if there were no children. Husbands sometimes exchanged wives for short periods of time and, as a mark of hospitality, even lent their wives to overnight visitors.

In much of the Arctic area, Eskimo religion was as simple as its social and political organization. There were no elaborate rituals and ceremonies, not even a girl's coming-out ceremony. The Eskimo believed that all things—plants, animals, rocks, sun, moon—had a soul or spirit. Sedna, the Sea Goddess, was perhaps the most important because she controlled the sea, the source of much of their food. In some places Moon Man was also important because he influenced game animals. To insure good hunting and ward off bad fortune the Eskimo observed numerous taboos and restrictions. Seal and deer meat, for example, couldn't be eaten together. To break this or one of the other taboos was a crime against the group.

To find out who had broken a taboo was one of the duties of the angakoks, the shamans or medicine men. In any Eskimo village shamans were the most important and influential individuals. Although women could become shamans, most were men.

The Eskimo developed shamanism to a high degree. Every village had several professional shamans. To impress the public with their powers they used ventriloquism, magic and sleight-of-hand tricks, including miraculously escapes after being tied hand and foot. Frequently the shaman would go into a trance as his special spirit-helper took possession of his body and spoke in a secret language. Or the shaman might send his own soul into the spirit world to get an answer to a question.

The shaman was expected to control the weather, foretell the future, find game or punish an enemy. But his main job was to cure disease. While doing this, he put on a good show, beating a tambourine, singing, dancing and working himself into a frenzy. Whether the patient lived or died, the shaman still collected his fee.

Along with many of their North American Indian neighbors, the Eskimo had a great fear of the ghosts of the dead. They didn't waste time disposing of the body. To confuse the ghost and prevent it from returning, they took the body out through a hole cut in the side of the house. Sometimes they plugged its nostrils with moss to keep the ghost in the body. The corpse was dressed in its Sunday best and wrapped or sewn inside a sealskin bag. Because of the frozen ground, they buried the body under a pile of rocks or left it on top of the ground.

Death was never far away from the Eskimo. Some groups were forced, in times of famine, to go off and abandon old people and cripples. This was not as cruel as it sounds. In fact, the old often requested to be left behind so they wouldn't be a burden on the others. If the Eskimo didn't abandon them, the entire group might die.

The Eskimo were not warlike. Small bands of Eskimo occasionally fought with some of their Athabascan neighbors over hunting or fishing grounds in the tundra. But they rarely fought with other Eskimo groups. Quarrels between individual Eskimo were, however, fairly common.

Courtesy, American Museum of Natural History
Skull over Eskimo grave, Port Clarence, Alaska

Most disputes were over women and often led to murder. Other arguments might be settled by satirical singing duels or by wrestling matches or fistfights.

Despite their nearly continual struggle for survival, the Eskimo enjoyed a good time. They were a jolly, cheerful people. They liked to amuse themselves during the long winter nights by feasting, by gambling with carved ivory dice or by listening to storytellers. They had a great many myths and folk tales which had been passed down from generation to generation. Some of these were believed to be true legends, while others were only for entertainment. The Eskimo also loved to sing, even holding song contests.

Today, after several centuries of contact with whalers, traders, missionaries and, within recent years, settlers, Eskimo life has changed. The gun had replaced the bow and arrow, the gasoline motor the paddle, the sewing machine the bone needle. Tea, coffee, sugar and flour have taken the place of many native foods, upsetting their former balanced diet. Nearly every house has its phonograph and stack of favorite American records to help pass away the time during the long winter nights.

Yet the old way of life hasn't entirely disappeared. Many Eskimo still live by hunting, trapping and fishing. Many still build snowhouses. Many still carve bone and ivory objects and decorate them with traditional designs.

12

The American Indian Today

THAT, THEN, is the story of the million North American Indians north of Mexico as they were at the time of their discovery by the first European explorers.

But what about the American Indian today?

How is he getting along in the atomic age? How has he adjusted to white civilization? Is he managing to hold his own? Or is he, like so many of his ancestors, well along the road to extinction?

In the first place, the Indians are far from vanishing. From a high of about one million when Columbus arrived, they hit bottom in the late nineteenth century. Epidemic disease, warfare and confinement on reservations all helped to cut their numbers by two-thirds. Many tribes were wiped out. Others were reduced to mere remnants. But since then they have bounced back until now they are perhaps the fastest growing cultural group in North America. Today there are nearly 800,000 Indians and Eskimo in the United States and Canada. Well over half a million live in 49 states, with slightly more than 200,000 in Canada.

According to the latest figures released by the Bureau of Indian Affairs, the largest centers of Indian population in the United States today are in Arizona with some 85,000, Oklahoma with 65,000, New Mexico with 56,000 and Alaska with about 42,000.

The largest single tribe in the United States and Canada is the Navaho of Arizona and New Mexico with a population of 100,000. The next largest is the Canadian Cree, with more than 46,000, followed closely by another Canadian tribe, the Ojibway, with over 42,000. In fourth place is the Siouan Dakota, most of whose 34,000 people live in North and South Dakota, with a few thousand stragglers in Minnesota, Nebraska and Canada. Strangely enough, all of these tribes are much larger today than they were when Europeans first invaded their territories.

Today most Indians live on reservations. A reservation is a tract of land, large or small, held in trust by the United States for the exclusive use of a particular group or groups of Indians. In 1962, there were over 300 separate areas occupied by Indians. They range in size from small settlements of a few acres in California up to the 25,000 square miles of the Navaho Reservation. In Canada, the Canadian Government has set aside 2,241 similar reserves for its Indians.

In the United States most of the Indians and their reservations are located west of the Mississippi River. There are still quite a number of Indians in the East—some Cherokees in North Carolina, Seminoles in Florida, Choctaws in Mississippi, Iroquois in New York, half a dozen tribes in Minnesota and Wisconsin, and a few others scattered here and there.

But the bulk of the Indians live in the western states. Some, like the Hopi and Navaho and other tribes of the Southwest, live on reservations within their ancient tribal boundaries. Others, like most of the two or three dozen tribes in Oklahoma, were gathered from all over the East and the Midwest, shoved into what was then called Indian Territory, and told to stay put.

In the last half of the nineteenth century some Indian reservations resembled concentration camps. Indians who had been at odds with the United States Government, such as the Dakota, Cheyenne, Comanche and various Apache tribes, were closely guarded, held almost as prisoners of war.

Until the Indians could get on their feet and begin to support themselves, they were furnished with food and clothing. But even here the Indians were frequently short-changed. More often than not they never received what they were supposed to get. Crooked Indian Agents and equally crooked contractors lined their pockets with the profits of delivering food hardly fit for hogs, shoddy blankets and other inferior supplies. The short rations, together with crowded conditions, brought on epidemic diseases—measles, diphtheria, smallpox, tuberculosis—all of which took their toll of lives.

As the Indian population declined and the white settlers on the frontier increased, the latter began demanding some of the reservation land. In one way or another, through wars or new treaties, many of the reservations were reduced in size, crowding the Indians still more.

The Indians were now urged to give up their old ways of life and become farmers instead of hunters. Tribes which had formerly lived by farming didn't have too much trouble. But the hunting tribes who had never raised food didn't like the idea. Besides, outside Arizona and New Mexico, farming was looked on as woman's work. To tell an Indian man to do woman's work was an insult. It was completely foreign to his way of thinking. So were most of the other white man's customs the Indians were supposed to adopt—living in wooden or log houses, wearing more clothes, cutting their hair short.

The last doesn't sound like much to get upset about. But to the Department of Indian Affairs it was one of the most important rules they laid down. To them long hair and braids were symbols of Indian ways. By cutting the Indian's hair they hoped to civilize him. Indian Agents were accordingly instructed not to hire an Indian until he had his hair cut short. The Indians, however, were proud of their braids and long hair, and most of them continued to wear their hair uncut.

Over the next half-century government policies toward the Indians changed from one administration to another. Some were good but others were bad. Under some the Indians prospered; under others they lost still more of their land.

During the last twenty or thirty years, however, things seem to be picking up for the Indians. The present Bureau of Indian Affairs states its objectives as (1) maximum

Indian economic self-sufficiency, (2) full participation of Indians in American life and (3) equal citizenship privileges and responsibilities for Indians. And the Bureau practices what it preaches. More than half its nearly 12,-000 regular employees have Indian blood.

Today, reservations are not concentration camps. The Indians are free to come and go as they please. Thousands and thousands of Indians live and work away from the reservations. These Indians are not wards of the government. In both the United States and Canada, Indians are citizens and are entitled to vote. Most Indian tribes govern themselves through tribal councils elected by the members of the tribe.

The government does not feed or take care of the Indians. Nor do Indians get pensions just because they are Indians. Like the rest of us, the Indians have to work for their living. Like us, they have to pay taxes unless exempted by treaty or other agreement. Like some of us, the elderly, the blind or other needy individuals receive public assistance or welfare. On reservations the government does provide education and health services for the Indians.

Just as there were differences in the ways the early Indians lived, so there are almost as great differences today. Some Indians in Oklahoma and elsewhere have become successful farmers; others, like the Western Apaches, successful cattle raisers. Some Indians are indifferent farmers or cattle raisers, barely managing to get by. The Northwest Coast Indians still live on salmon, but most of them now work in salmon canneries or on fishing boats.

In Canada and Alaska bands of Indian and Eskimo hunters and trappers continue to roam their old homelands. Hundreds of Iroquois braves have become famous as structural steel workers on high buildings and bridges from New York to San Francisco.

Nearly everywhere the ancient way of Indian life is changing, sometimes slowly, sometimes rapidly. Yet there is little danger that it will disappear entirely, at least not for a great many years. Some tribes, like the Hopi and Zuñi, even after four hundred years of contact with European civilization, still live much like their ancestors did in 1540. They inhabit the same stone-walled apartment houses, till the same small patches of corn, beans and squash, and perform the same old ceremonies, including their famed Snake Dance. Many Navaho Indians also still cling to many of their traditional beliefs and values. The Western Apaches still put on their spectacular coming-out ceremony for girls. Among the Iroquois in New York, the False Face Society still gives its grotesquely masked rituals.

Nor are native arts and crafts things of the past. Some tribes still make pottery and basketry and other implements and utensils for their own use. But many have capitalized on the tourist demand for anything made by Indians and have gone into the curio business. The Pueblo Indians make fine pottery for sale. But they have modernized their typical bowl and jar shapes and also turn out ashtrays, lamps, candlesticks and other special forms. From the wool of their own sheep Navaho women weave fine rugs and blankets while their husbands make equally fine turquoise and silver jewelry. Basketmaking for tourists is a thriving industry among the Pima and Papago and a number of other tribes. Using modern beads and age-old designs, many Indians make beaded belts, headbands, moccasins and other articles. In northern Canada modern Eskimo are continuing the excellent stone and ivory carving of their ancestors, and developing new forms of stone carving.

Most Indian tribes formerly painted designs on skins or wood or pottery. Today some of their descendants are using paper and canvas to preserve ancient tribal rituals and ways of everyday life. This uniquely American style of painting is being carried on by artists of a dozen different tribes—Hopi, Zia Pueblo, Santa Clara Pueblo, Jemez Pueblo, San Ildefonso Pueblo, Navaho, Apache, Dakota, Cheyenne, Comanche, Kiowa and Creek. The names of many of these Indian painters, both men and women, are becoming well-known throughout the art world. Their paintings are exhibited in museums and art galleries all over the world.

Some Indian tribes, like the Navaho and Osage, have made money through discoveries of oil, natural gas, helium or uranium on their reservations. The income from mineral resources through rentals and royalties was more than $41 million during the 1963 fiscal year. The Indians made another $8 million from the sale of timber cut on reservations. Other tribes, like the Western Apaches and their cousins, the Mescalero Apaches, have gone into the recreation business and built gas stations, motels and hunting and fishing lodges. Canadian Indians make several million dollars each year from trapping beaver, muskrat and other fur-bearing animals. Some Indians of Manitoba have made a good thing out of catching frogs for United States markets.

Yet most Indians, in comparison to their white neighbors, are still poor. In 1959 the average per-capita income in the United States was $2,159. For the same year the average Indian had an income of only $500.

The descendants of these Indian discoverers of North America have much for which they can be proud. They were the first Americans. They were the first to discover and develop the resources of the New World. For this we owe them a great deal.

Just think what our menus would be like without corn on the cob and cornflakes and popcorn and all the other varieties of corn and beans and other native foods. If the Indians hadn't developed any food plants, we would have a lot less to eat. Plants first domesticated by the Indians today furnish almost half the world's supply of food.

Our clothes wouldn't be the same without the Indians. The commercial cottons of the world come chiefly from types first cultivated by the Indians. All that we raise in the United States is of American Indian origin. So also is the long-fiber cotton now grown in Egypt and other parts of Africa.

Another plant the Indians gave to us, one that we aren't yet sure we should thank them for, is tobacco.

The Indian's contribution to our way of life didn't stop with plants. We borrowed their birchbark canoes, their snowshoes and toboggans, their tipis and wigwams, their pueblo style of architecture, their games such as lacrosse, their ideas of democracy.

We even borrowed hundreds of Indian words to add to our language, including such words as caucus, coyote, hominy, maize, moose, papoose, squaw, succotash, tipi, tobacco, toboggan and wigwam.

Over half our states have Indian names. Among them are Arizona, Connecticut, North and South Dakota, Illinois, Kentucky, Massachusetts, Michigan, Mississippi, Missouri, Nebraska, Ohio, Texas and Wyoming. The number of cities with Indian names is even greater—Cheyenne, Chicago, Hackensack, Kalamazoo, Keokuk, Minneapolis, Mobile, Niagara, Omaha, Oshkosh, Pensacola, Schenectady, Seattle, Tacoma, Tallahassee, Topeka and Wichita. Names of lakes, rivers, mountains and other landmarks could be added to the list.

In Canada there is the same story of borrowing. Seven of its provinces and districts owe to the Indians their present names.

Today we recognize the prominent place the Indians had in our nation's development. All across the country a score or more of our national parks and monuments protect and preserve the sites of ancient Indian towns. Our museums are crowded with pottery and basketry and other implements and utensils showing the artistry and skill of both the prehistoric and historic Indians. Archaeologists are still digging, still finding more to add to our knowledge about the Indians.

The story of the American Indian has not ended. His

way of life may be on its eventual way out. But for centuries to come these parks and monuments and museum exhibits will stand as memorials to the great debt we owe these first Americans.

Bibliography

Baldwin, Gordon C., *America's Buried Past*. New York, G. P. Putnam's Sons, 1962.

———— *The Ancient Ones*. New York, W. W. Norton & Company, Inc., 1963.

———— *The Warrior Apaches*. Globe, Arizona, Dale Stuart King, 1965.

———— *Stone Age Peoples Today*. New York, W. W. Norton & Company, Inc., 1964.

Cooke, David C., *Fighting Indians of the West*. New York, Dodd, Mead & Company, 1954.

Driver, Harold C., *Indians of North America*. Chicago, University of Chicago Press, 1961.

Douglas, Frederic H., and D'Harnoncourt, Rene, *Indian Art of the United States*. New York, The Museum of Modern Art, 1941.

Drucker, Philip, *Indians of the Northwest Coast*. Garden City, New York, The Natural History Press, 1963.

Ewers, John C., *The Blackfeet*. Norman, Oklahoma, The University of Oklahoma Press, 1958.

Hagan, William T., *American Indians*. Chicago, The University of Chicago Press, 1961.

Hibben, Frank C., *Treasure in the Dust*. Philadelphia, J. B. Lippincott Company, 1951.

Jenness, Diamond, *The Indians of Canada*. Ottawa, Queen's Printer, Fourth Edition, 1958.

———— *The People of the Twilight*. Chicago, The University of Chicago Press, 1959.

Josephy, A. M., Jr., ed., *The American Heritage Book of Indians*. New York, American Heritage Publishing Company, Inc., 1961.

———— *The Patriot Chiefs*. New York, The Viking Press, Inc., 1961.

LaFarge, Oliver, *A Pictorial History of the American Indian*. New York, Crown, 1956.

Leavitt, Jerome E., *America and Its Indians*. New York, Grosset & Dunlap, 1962.

216

Lowie, Robert H., *Indians of the Plains*. Garden City, New York, The Natural History Press, 1963.

Lyford, Carrie A., *Iroquois Crafts*. Phoenix, Phoenix Indian School, 1945.

MacGowan, Kenneth, and Hester, Joseph A., Jr., *Early Man in the New World*, rev. ed. Garden City, New York, The Natural History Press, 1962.

Marriott, Alice, *Saynday's People*. Lincoln, The University of Nebraska Press, 1963.

Mead, Margaret, *People and Places*. New York, Bantam Books, 1963.

Morris, Anne Axtell, *Digging in the Southwest*. New York, Doubleday, Doran & Company, 1933.

Newcomb, W. W., Jr., *The Indians of Texas*. Austin, The University of Texas Press, 1961.

Quimby, George I., *Indian Life in the Upper Great Lakes*. Chicago, The University of Chicago Press, 1960.

Raphael, Ralph B., *Book of American Indians*. New York, Arco Publishing Company, 1960.

Silverberg, Robert, *Home of the Red Man*. Greenwich, Connecticut, New York Graphic Society, 1963.

Stirling, M. W., ed., *Indians of the Americas*. Washington, The National Geographic Society, 1961.

Tschopik, Harry, Jr., *Indians of North America*. New York, The American Museum of Natural History, 1952.

Underhill, Ruth M., *Pueblo Crafts*. Phoenix, Phoenix Indian School, 1945.

———— *Red Man's America*. Chicago, The University of Chicago Press, 1953.

Wallace, Ernest, and Hoebel, E. Adamson, *The Comanches*. Norman, Oklahoma, The University of Oklahoma Press, 1952.

Wedel, Waldo R., *Prehistoric Man on the Great Plains*. Norman, Oklahoma, The University of Oklahoma Press, 1961.

Wissler, Clark, *The American Indian*. New York, Oxford University Press, 1938.

———— *Indians of the United States*. Garden City, New York, Doubleday, Doran & Company, 1940.

Glossary

Anasazi—Navaho Indian word meaning "the Ancient Ones," the prehistoric Basket Maker and Pueblo Indians of the Southwest.

Angakok—An Eskimo shaman or medicine man.

Anthropology—The study of man and his culture.

Archaeology—The study of the material remains of ancient peoples before written records.

Artifact—Archaeological term for any object made by man.

Awl—A pointed implement, usually of bone, for boring holes in skins or other materials.

Basket Maker—A prehistoric group of Indians living nearly 2000 years ago in the Four Corners area of Arizona, New Mexico, Colorado and Utah.

Carbon 14 dating—A method of determining the age of archaeological materials of organic origin by measuring the amount of breakdown of the carbon 14 atoms.

Clan—A social unit based on kinship which is counted through one parent only.

Culture—In an anthropological sense, the implements and utensils and other remains showing how a particular people lived.

Culture area—A geographical area in which the cultures tend to be one general type.

Dendrochronology—The dating of prehistoric ruins by means of the wet and dry sequences in the annual rings of certain trees.

Flint—A variety of quartz, as chert, chalcedony or jasper, used by many Indians for their chipped stone implements.

Folsom point—A fluted spear or dart point used by prehistoric Indians to hunt buffalo and other big game.

Harpoon—A spear with a detachable head tied to a long line.

Hohokam—The Pima Indian word for the ancient peoples of southern Arizona.

Kayak—The Eskimo one-man skin boat.

218

Kinship—The classification of relatives.

Kiva—The ceremonial chamber, usually underground, of the Pueblo Indians.

Manitou—Algonkian Indian term for the supernatural power present in all things.

Mano—The hand grinding stone used for grinding corn or other material on a metate.

Matrilineal—Descent traced through the female line.

Metate—The stone slab on which the mano is rubbed to grind corn or seeds.

Mogollon—An early agricultural, pottery-making culture in eastern Arizona and western New Mexico.

Mound Builders—Prehistoric Indians of the eastern United States who built burial or temple mounds.

Obsidian—Volcanic glass used by many Indians for arrowheads and other chipped implements.

Patayan—A prehistoric culture along the Colorado River in western Arizona.

Patrilineal—Descent traced through the male line.

Pemmican—An Indian food made of dried and pulverized meat mixed with melted fat and dried berries.

Piki—Hopi Indian wafer bread made of ground cornmeal.

Pinole—A Southwestern Indian drink made of ground roasted cornmeal mixed with water.

Potlatch—A Northwest Coast Indian ceremony in which property was given away or destroyed.

Pottery—Bowls, jars and other vessels made of fired clay.

Pueblo—The Spanish word for town and used by anthropologists to refer to certain Southwestern Indians and their stone and adobe apartment houses.

Salado—Prehistoric Southwestern Indians, a mixture of Anasazi and Mogollon peoples.

Shaman—Siberian word for a medicine man.

Site—Any place that shows signs of human occupation, such as houses, pottery fragments, stone implements, bones, etc.

Tipi—An Indian hut made of a conical framework of poles covered with skins.

Tribe—A group of people usually having a common name for themselves, a common language, definite territory and a common culture.

Umiak—The Eskimo skin-covered woman's boat.

Wampum—Strings of shell beads often used as money by many of the Eastern Indians and early white settlers.

Wigwam—The Algonkian Indian word for a circular, dome-shaped, birchbark-covered house.

Index

221

The Author

DR. GORDON C. BALDWIN worked his way through universities by putting together broken fragments of pottery for the Arizona State Museum. There were enough fragments and enough Baldwin perseverance to achieve a B.A. in Anthropology at the University of Arizona and a Ph.D. at the University of Southern California. Since then Dr. Baldwin has devoted a lifetime to studying, teaching, practicing, and writing about archaeology. His writings include scientific articles, adult western novels, and juvenile nonfiction books. For Putnam's he has authored *Race Against Time: The Story of Salvage Archaeology, America's Buried Past: The Story of North American Archaeology,* and *The World of Prehistory: The Story of Man's Beginnings.*